The American
Immigration Collection

The Story
of a
Bohemian-American
Village

ROBERT I. KUTAK

Arno Press and The New York Times

NEW YORK · 1970

71- 1124

Reprint Edition 1970 by Arno Press Inc.

Reprinted from a copy in
The Columbia University Library

LC# 70-129406
ISBN 0-405-00559-8

The American Immigration Collection—Series II
ISBN for complete set 0-405-00543-1

Manufactured in the United States of America

The Story of
A BOHEMIAN-AMERICAN VILLAGE

A Study of Social Persistence and Change

By

ROBERT I. KUTAK

*Assistant Professor of Sociology,
University of Louisville*

*Submitted in partial fulfillment of the requirements
for the degree of Doctor of Philosophy, in the Faculty of Political Science, Columbia University*

THE STANDARD PRINTING COMPANY
INCORPORATED
LOUISVILLE, KENTUCKY
1933

PREFACE

Without the co-operation of the people of Milligan this study could not have been made. The author is greatly indebted to the inhabitants, Czech and non-Czech alike, who gave frank and honest answers to the many questions asked them. In previous visits the author had made many friends in the Milligan community. Among these Mr. Charles Smrha, Dr. V. V. Smrha, Mr. James Charvat, and Mr. J. J. Klima gave many constructive suggestions and helped pave the way for the visits to the households. The unfailing interest and constructive advice of Dr. Jaroslav Novak, Czechoslovak Consul General in New York, and Mr. E. F. Prantner, former editor of the *Czechoslovak Review* have aided the author greatly in his task.

This study developed out of a report given in the seminar conducted by Professor A. A. Tenney. It is based on the sociological system of Professor R. M. MacIver, whose penetrating books are indispensable to an understanding of social life. The author is indebted to Professors R. E. Chaddock, R. S. Lynd, and F. A. Ross for many helpful suggestions. Without the assistance of his wife the author could not have completed this book.

R. I. K.

May 1, 1933

INTRODUCTION

For several years before making the study of Milligan described in the following chapters the author was interested in the problem of the adjustment of the Czech immigrant to American life. His father and mother were both born in Bohemia. In his own family he had an opportunity to observe the process of adjustment to life in the new world. As he grew older he wondered how the adjustment was made in other Czech families in America.

In 1928 the author entered upon graduate study in the Department of Sociology at Columbia University. In a seminar conducted by Professor A. A. Tenney he read a paper on the adjustment of the Czech immigrant to urban and rural life in the United States. At Professor Tenney's suggestion he decided to make this problem the subject of his dissertation. The plan of study first drawn up included a year's study of the folkways of the Bohemia from which the immigrants had come, an extensive study of the adjustments made in various communities in America, and an intensive study of one such community. It was soon discovered that this plan was too ambitious, and it was decided to make the intensive study of immigrant adjustment in a single rural community the subject of the dissertation. The other parts of the plan were left for future research.

While at Columbia the author became very much interested in the sociological concepts of Professor R. M. MacIver, particularly those which deal with social change. The present study attempts to explore this field with the sociological system of Professor MacIver as a compass.

Purposes of Study

In making this study the investigator had two purposes in mind. The first was to discover which modes of behavior had persisted in the new world and which had changed, and, in so far as possible, to discover the causes of these persistences and changes. The second purpose was to discover whether or not the adjustment of a group of Czech immigrants to a country environment in the new world differed from that made to a city environment in America. A large proportion of recent immigrants have settled in cities. Most of them were peasants who came from a country village in Europe to a city in America. The new life which they were forced to live presented many difficulties and raised many problems. How much of the difficulty was due to the fact that the immigrants came from one national culture to another, and how much to the fact that they came from a country to a city environment? Are not a good many of the so-called problems of immigration really problems of urbanization? An attempt to answer these questions is made in the study here presented.

In the course of this investigation data were secured on the reactions of a group of country-bred Czech people to a country environment in America. In 1920 Jakub Horak presented a Ph. D. dissertation at the University of Chicago[1] which treated of the adjustment of country-bred Czechs to life in an American city. In these two studies the factor of nationality has been held constant. It is logical to assume that the differences between the two types of Czech communities in the new world will be caused mainly by the fact that in one case the community is located in the country and in the other case it is located in the city. Some tentative conclusions may be drawn with respect to the part which urbanization plays in the creation of problems of immigrant adjustment to American life. It is too often assumed that there is but one American way of life, whereas actually there are two Americas, one rural and the other urban. The type of adjustment which immigrants make is conditioned by the America to which they come. A comparison of two communities, one rural and the other urban, would lead to greater understanding of the problems involved in the adjustment of immigrants to the new world.

Methodology

Milligan, Nebraska, was selected as the community to be studied because it is an isolated rural community and because the investigator was already acquainted with its social life. For some years before the study was made the author had paid periodic visits to the village. He passed the summer of 1919 visiting the family of the village banker. Every two or three years thereafter he returned for a brief visit. Thus he was well acquainted with the village, and had in advance of the study a general idea of the modes of behavior which would probably exhibit great persistence, and those which had proved most responsive to change.

The investigator conducted the study during July and August of 1930. He used two sets of schedules, one individual and one household, consisting of questions which would bring out evidences of persistence and change in the modes of behavior of the Czech inhabitants.

[1] Jakub Horak, *Assimilation of Czechs in Chicago*, unpublished Ph. D. dissertation, University of Chicago, 1920.

It was discovered early in the study that little use could be made of census data. The Census Bureau does not give detailed data for villages as small as Milligan. Moreover, such data could not be secured for the community as a whole. A total of approximately 1,100 people live in the Milligan community. In 1930, 412 of these lived in the village, while about 700 lived in the country surrounding Milligan. The village is located about one mile from the boundary line between Fillmore and Saline counties. Some of the inhabitants of the community thus live in one county, some in the other. Detailed data for townships would have been useless, as the community includes nearly all of Glengary township and parts of a number of other townships. It was necessary thus to rely almost entirely upon the data which could be gathered in the course of the investigation.

Because the investigator had to rely greatly upon data which he had gathered, it was necessary to make sure that the sample of the population to be visited would be adequate to serve as a basis for conclusions. Because the population living in the village was relatively heterogeneous, it was felt that it would be necessary to visit every home in order to secure adequate data. Data were secured from 128 of 134 homes in the village. In three of the homes the members refused to answer any questions. In two of them lived feeble old widows who could not understand the questions. In one of them an elderly grandmother was dying of cancer, and the investigator did not wish to disturb the other members of the family. The population living on the farms surrounding Milligan is much more homogeneous. It was believed that data from about one-third of the farms would be an adequate sample. The farms to be visited were selected at random. Out of a total of about 200 farm families, 72 were visited and data secured. Of the 200 families visited in the community as a whole, 18 were non-Czech, while in five cases one of the parents was Czech and the other non-Czech. Of the 177 families in which both parents were Czech, the head of the family was of first-generation stock in 101 cases and of second-generation stock in 76 cases. The families visited are summarized in Table I.

TABLE I
HOUSEHOLD SCHEDULES CLASSIFIED

	Head First Gen.	Head Second Gen.	Non-Czech	One Parent Czech—one Non-Czech	Total
In Village	71	40	12	5	128
Farms	30	36	6	0	72
Total	101	76	18	5	200

In the 200 households visited lived a total of 681 people. Three hundred and thirteen of these lived in first-generation homes, 290 in second-generation homes, 62 in non-Czech homes, and 16 in homes in which one parent was Czech and one parent was non-Czech. Of the 681 people, 389 lived in the village and 292 lived on the farm. If the 681 people are grouped according to ages, it is found that 253 are under twenty-one, 264 are between twenty-one and thirty-nine inclusive, and 164 are forty and over.

Individual schedules were not filled out for all of the 681 people living in the households. It was discovered that children under twelve and some of the older people were unable to understand many of the questions that were asked. In some instances the individuals were absent when the investigator visited the household. Individual schedules were filled out in whole or in part for 561 persons living in the community. Nearly all of the 120 persons for whom individual schedules were not filled out were children under twelve. Three hundred and seventeen of those for whom schedules were filled out lived in the village and 244 lived on the farm. Of the 52 non-Czechs, 31 lived in the village and 21 on the farm. The distribution of the 509 Czechs by age, sex, and generation is given in Table II. Of the 509 Czechs for whom individual schedules were filled out 286 lived in the village and 223 lived on the farm. Those who lived in the village included 100 of the first generation, 145 of the second generation, and 41 of the third. On the farm were found 40 of the first generation, 122 of the second, and 61 of the third.

TABLE II

CZECH INDIVIDUALS CLASSIFIED BY AGE, SEX, AND GENERATION

Age Group	First Gen. Men	First Gen. Women	First Gen. Total	Second Gen. Men	Second Gen. Women	Second Gen. Total	Third Gen. Men	Third Gen. Women	Third Gen. Total
12-20	0	0	0	32	37	69	24	23	47
21-39	6	4	10	61	58	119	31	24	55
40 plus	69	61	130	39	40	79	0	0	0
Total	75	65	140	132	135	267	55	47	102

While schedules were filled out for 561 persons, not all of them answered all of the questions. Some would not answer certain of the questions, while others could not. These individuals never constituted more than 12 per cent of the total number for whom schedules were filled out.

The two sets of schedules were filled out by the investigator for each household at the time he made his visit. In many of the households the members could not speak the English language. In those cases the investigator translated the Czech answers into English.

A second source of data was to be found in the files of the village and county newspapers.[2] About ten years before the study was made the village newspaper was consolidated with the county newspaper. Some of the old issues of the village newspaper were available, however, and were utilized by the investigator. The county newspaper has been published as long as Milligan has been incorporated as a village. In each issue for a number of years a considerable amount of space has been devoted to events which concerned Milligan.

Schedules and newspapers offer much valuable data, but do not tell all there is to know about changes in the modes of behavior in a community over a period of years. In dealing with the folkways of a community an important method which must be pursued is the observational. The subtle inner aspects of the social life of a community cannot be deduced from hard facts and cold figures. The investigator must participate in the life of the community, must enter into the social relationships of the people. Only so can he really observe what goes on in the community life. The investigator spent considerable time attending dances and funerals, sitting on the benches in front of the stores on Main Street or in the soft-drink parlors, visiting professional men in their offices, eating lunches and dinners with the townspeople and the farmers.

These intangible yet highly important aspects of community life cannot be gotten at with schedules and questionnaires, nor can one describe them with statistical tables. The investigator made a definite attempt to get the "feel" and "flavor" of the community life, and he has tried to portray these aspects in the course of this book. Sociology is a science, and like all sciences it must be sure of its facts. However, it is a unique science, in that it treats of social living, which is an art. Hence art and science must be combined in the presentation of its data or sociology fails to realize the objective toward which all science strives, to tell the truth about the subject matter with which it deals.

In order to assist in giving the feel of the community a number of quotations are given. These quotations do not form the basis of the conclusions reached, but are offered as a means of showing the inner aspects of the life of the com-

[2] *Nebraska Signal*, published at Geneva, and the *Milligan Times*.

munity. They give an opportunity for the people to tell in their own words how the community and its changes affect them. They also show the real diversity of opinion that there is within the community. "Typical" answers serve a useful purpose in that they show what the "public" opinion in a community is, but they never tell the whole story, or even a large part of it.

With the data that he has gathered the writer believes that he has been able to accomplish the purposes of his study. Chapter XII summarizes the data, and points out which aspects of the community life have shown the greatest persistence and which have been most responsive to change. A comparison is made of the life of the Czechs of Milligan with that lived by Czechs who settled in Chicago. In Milligan the Czechs control their own destinies pretty largely and are confronted with few of the problems which cause maladjustment among their brothers in Chicago. Further studies should be made to determine what part immigration and what part urbanization play in the causation of the problems which confront immigrants who settle in cities.

General Description of Milligan Community

Milligan is located in the southeastern part of Nebraska. It is 60 miles due west of Lincoln, the state capital, and about 50 miles north of the Kansas border. A mile east of Milligan is the boundary between Fillmore County, in which Milligan is situated, and the adjoining county, Saline.

The earliest settlers in the Milligan community began to arrive soon after the Civil War. By 1887 this section of Nebraska was relatively thickly populated, and the Kansas City & Omaha Railroad believed that it would be profitable to build a branch line from Fairbury to McCool Junction. At intervals of 15 or 20 miles along the line villages were established. Milligan was one of these villages. On February 15, 1888, the village was duly organized and incorporated, with two Czechs and three Americans on its first board of trustees. It grew rapidly in its early years, and by 1900 was able to report that "The various lines of trade and business have so developed that at present it is possible to procure all the necessities of life at home."[3] In this year the village listed 83 families, of which 69 were of Czech extraction. All of the village officials in this year were Czech.

The population of Milligan continued to increase until 1920, when the Census Bureau reported 418 inhabitants. Pop-

---

[3] F. B. Matlack and F. A. Stech, *History of the Village of Milligan* (Omaha, 1900), p. 16.

ulation changes in the village, township, and county in recent
years as given by the Census Bureau are shown in Table III.

TABLE III

POPULATION CHANGES, 1910-1930, MILLIGAN VILLAGE, GLENGARY TOWNSHIP, AND FILLMORE COUNTY

	Number of Inhabitants		
	1910	1920	1930
Milligan Village	336	418	412
Glengary Township	909	951	915
Fillmore County	14,674	13,671	12,971

About 1,100 people lived in the Milligan community in
1930. Ninety per cent of them were of Czech extraction. The
others were of old American, Irish, Swedish, or German descent. The 412 people in the village lived in 134 households.
The 700 who occupied the farms lived in 200 households.[4]

In 1930 the village had an assessed valuation of $364,-
455.58. The total bonded debt, $29,600, was rather large for
a Nebraska village as small as Milligan. The seven blocks of
paved streets accounted for $21,500 of this debt.[5]

Business establishments in Milligan include two general
stores, one grocery, one hardware store, two furniture stores,
one drug store, two barber shops, two blacksmith shops, four
garages, one real estate office, two restaurants, one hotel, one
bank, three grain elevators, two combination theatres and
dance halls, one meat market, one coal and lumber dealer,
one shoe-repair shop, three soft-drink parlors, one implement
dealer, one machine shop, one hatchery, and three cream-
receiving stations. There is one doctor, and one dentist
who divides his time between Milligan and Geneva, the county
seat.

The land about Milligan is fairly level. On it the farmers
raise wheat, corn, alfalfa, and livestock.

In this setting the people pass their lives. A picture of
the changing life of the community is given in the chapters
of this book.

---

[4] In the course of the study 129 villages and 72 farm households were visited.   See Table I
p. ix.
[5] Data furnished by Fillmore County treasurer.

TABLE OF CONTENTS

LIST OF TABLES

CHAPTER I

A BIRD'S EYE VIEW

Milligan, "the Bohemian town with the Irish name," lies about sixty miles west of Lincoln, Nebraska, some two hours away if one travels by automobile, but a much greater distance by train. The fact that Milligan was founded by a railroad suggests accessibility. Unfortunate indeed is the poor traveler who acts upon this belief.

At Fairmont, an hour distant from Lincoln, one leaves the main line of the railroad to take the local to Milligan. None of the trains on the main line makes a connection with the Milligan branch and hence it is necessary to come to the village of Fairmont the evening before and spend the night at its ancient and dilapidated hotel. Its star has been waning since the advent of the automobile made accessible to traveling salesmen the hotels in the larger towns nearby.

In the morning a combination freight and passenger train leaves Fairmont for Milligan and other towns beyond. The passengers sit in a small and dirty compartment at one end of the baggage car. At each town and village the train stops for an interminable period while the engine shunts box cars about. The train maintains its schedule about as well as did the Italian railroads before the days of Mussolini.

Happily for the traveler, it is quite easy now to escape the terrors of both hotel and train. Salesmen are not the only ones who have profited by the invention of the automobile. A gravel road leads from Fairmont to Milligan, and for a nominal sum the visitor will be carried in the rickety old Ford touring car which serves as village taxicab and deposited at the hotel on Main Street in Milligan.

A few years ago Main Street was a muddy thoroughfare during the rainy season, and a dusty one at all other times; but today the four blocks along which the business houses are located are paved with concrete. Three of the side streets have likewise been paved, and Milligan boasts proudly that it is the smallest town in the state with paved streets. Its inhabitants have had to pay a heavy toll in order to be able to make this boast, and some of them grumble considerably over taxes. The progressive spirit that produced the paved streets also replaced the wooden buildings on the west side of Main Street with new brick structures. The largest of these buildings is the new auditorium, erected in 1930, with funds raised by the various Czech lodges of the village. It is the center of the social life of the town, and young and old come from far and near to attend the dances and other entertainments held there. Wherever Czech people are to be found, the "síň" or hall serves as the social agency which unifies the community and in which the people's habits of sociability have opportunity for expression.

Central Hall, the old "opera house," dominates the east side of Main Street. This barn-like structure was built thirty-five years ago and contains memories of the social life of three generations. In former days the front room of the hall was a saloon. The long bar is still in use, but on its mahogany top is served no longer the "pivo" which the Czechs of the village love so much. In front of the bar are several tables at which men sit playing cards or discussing the affairs of the community and of the world.

Most of the men in the group are old. Born in Bohemia, they came to Nebraska in the late decades of the nineteenth century and spent a lifetime tilling the soil. Many of them use only the Czech language, but find this no handicap in the Milligan community, as nearly everyone understands them when they speak their native tongue.

"How much is wheat selling for?"

"The elevators here paid sixty-two cents today (July 5, 1930). Ain't it terrible the way the price of wheat has gone down? Wheat has been up and down before, but I ain't ever seen it go down as quick as it has this time, and I've been farming in this country for sixty-five years. How are the farmers going to meet their interest, pay taxes, and buy anything if this keeps up?"

"I guess times are bad, but then we shouldn't complain. We must take things as they come, the bad along with the good. Everything will come out all right in the long run."

The members of the group agree with the last speaker, and seem to be resigned to conditions as they are. Calm acceptance of the blows of fate seems to be characteristic of the Czech peasant. This attitude is not found among the second- and third-generation Czechs; these continually reach for a more expensive standard of living.

Prohibition suggests another topic of conversation.

"Gee, but I wish I had a cold glass of beer. America's not what it used to be. We came here to get liberty and freedom, and what do they give us? Near beer and pop. It ain't even fit for women and children to drink."

"What are you complaining for? Your old woman makes better beer than any brewery ever made. Before prohibition we had two or three kinds of beer for all people to drink. Now every home makes its own beer, and makes the kind it likes. I don't like the idea of prohibition, but we haven't had it yet."

"That's all right, but I like to go up to a bar to get my beer. Also, look at what prohibition has done to our taxes. Before prohibition we had three saloons in Milligan. Each paid a thousand dollars a year for a license, and there were no taxes. Today we have no saloons and high taxes. It ain't right."

"Our taxes are high today because we've made so many improvements. If we keep on at this rate we'll all go broke."

"Well, if we do all go to the poorhouse, we'll have paved streets and graveled roads to travel over in getting there. I don't think we've made near enough improvements yet. We've got one of the best small towns in the state, and we live like human beings instead of like cattle. There are lots of things we need. The kids would enjoy a swimming pool and a playground, and we older people could use a library."

"The kids have it too easy as it is. Make 'em work, is what I say. Why, all they want is to ride around in cars and have a good time and spend money. Prohibition is responsible for it. Bring back the saloon, and they'll stop drinking."

"There's nothing wrong with the young folks. They are no different than we were. They like to have a good time, but so did we when we were young. We've got as fine a lot of young folks as you'd find anywhere in the country."

The group at the tables in the saloon does not dwell for any length of time on the misbehavior of the young. Old people are usually interested in the aged, and especially in those of the aged who are ill.

"I hear old man Svec is very sick. My neighbor tells me that they don't expect him to live much longer."

"Yes, that's true. It won't be long now before he'll move out to the cemetery. He's eighty-five years old, and can't expect to live forever. It won't be long now before I'll be gone too; I'm nearly as old as he is. I can remember when old man Svec was young man Svec. He once owned the land on which Milligan now stands. We had some real hard times back in those days. Things are better now."

"What we need most of all in Milligan is a factory. There is no work to be had around here. Our young people leave the town and go to the city to work. If we had a factory, they would remain here and the town would grow."

The last proposition is one to which there is no opposition. The town is finding it difficult to keep its young people, and a factory manufacturing cream cheese or other milk products and employing workmen would keep the young at home and furnish a new market for the business men. Nearly all of the towns in this section of Nebraska are in a similar situation, and each hopes to solve its difficulty by the establishment of a factory.

While problems of human life and destiny are being settled inside the hall, interested groups occupy the benches which line both sides of Main Street and listen to the program being broadcast from the village radio station. The benches are usually occupied in the daytime by the older men who gossip away the hours as the sun travels slowly across the heavens. In the morning they use those on the east side of the street, and in the afternoon they follow the shade across to the benches on the west. In the evening most of them yield their benches to the youth of the village and to farmers who have come in from the country, and gather in the more convivial atmosphere of Central Hall. Such is the daily life of those who have retired; this Nirvana is the aim and end of all Milliganites who earn their living by the sweat of their brow.

The village radio station is in the room above the former saloon. For many years the room has served as a lodge room. On its walls are hung the charters of the various lodges, and the pictures of men who have figured prominently in the history of Bohemia and America. The kind and gentle face of Hus hangs beside the granite-like countenance of McKinley, while on the opposite wall the fires of idealism shine alike in the eyes of Wilson and Masaryk. It has been many years since the room was last cleaned, and the dust of time lies upon everything. Battered pieces of lodge equipment are scattered about the floor. The breeze coming through the south windows barely disturbs the stifling atmosphere. The heat in the room is very oppressive.

Into this old room with its musty atmosphere there has been introduced a new note. In one corner stands an amplifier, which may be used to broadcast announcements and the music of phonograph records, as well as to amplify radio programs picked off the air. During the course of several years attempts were made to organize a band to play on nights when the stores are open for the trade of farmers from the surrounding country. These attempts proved unsuccessful, and the village banker hit upon the idea of a village radio station as a means of interesting the farmers. For a year the loudspeakers on the roof outside have blared forth their programs on "open nights," and throngs have come to listen and to buy.

The village banker is the announcer and director of the ceremonies. In the Czech language he extols the virtues of the banana.

"Friends and neighbors, I bring you a message on this hot night that you will be glad to receive. One of the greatest difficulties which we have to face in this tropical weather is the choice of food to eat. Roast pork and dumplings are excellent foods, but not for a stomach that is already overheated. Why not turn to the tropics for the things to eat in this hot weather? The banana is a tropical fruit. What could be a better food in such heat as we have had lately? The banana can be eaten at all hours of the day. It is an excellent breakfast fruit. Those of you who farm can take it to the fields with you, and eat it when you are hungry. Charlie Kotas foresaw what kind of weather we were going to have, and has thoughtfully provided you with an opportunity to purchase this unexcelled fruit. You may buy it at his store. Come early, as his bananas will soon be gone."

Before the evening is over all the bananas are sold, and a worried store proprietor will sleep in peace, certain that his large supply will not spoil on his hands.

Advertising, no matter how eloquent, would soon pall on the listeners. The next number is a phonograph record containing a humorous Czech dialogue. The shouts of laughter which ring out in the street below testify to the appreciation of the audience. After this one of the girls of the neighborhood plays a rollicking Czech dance melody on the accordion. This number receives great applause. The members of the audience would rather listen to Czech music than eat.

Again the voice of the announcer is heard advertising a product sold in the stores.

"I have been asked to call your attention to a product which is carried by all the grocery stores in town. I do not know what the article is used for, but I have been informed that it comes in handy when the wife wishes to make bread. It is made of malt and hops, and it is called 'Pra Zdroj.' Step into the nearest store and get yourself some of this wonderful preparation."

A special number is given next. It consists of a song about Milligan and its greatness written by the town poet. It is sung with deep feeling by several of the boys. One of the men sitting on the curb remarks, "Gee, they're certainly giving the town a big boost in that song."

Another Czech record is played, after which the announcer calls the attention of his audience to a serious problem confronting the town:

"I have been informed that there is no room to park on the paved streets. I am sure there will be room enough for all if everyone is careful to park as near to the next car as possible. Will you all please pay careful attention to this request?"[1]

Many farmers have come to town this evening to patronize the stores on this "open night." On these evenings the brightly-lighted store windows of Main Street look out upon a busy throng of men, women, and children, hurrying from one place to another, buying prodigious amounts of food and clothing. On the street outside the store fronts fat rosy-cheeked farmer wives stand and gossip, while their children at play make life miserable for those who drive up and down Main Street. The men of the family gather at Central Hall to play cards and discuss the crops and the economic situation. On Main Street farmers meet and hire harvest hands. Many itinerant workers are in town looking for jobs. This is a bad year for them, however, as the local help is almost sufficient to finish the work of harvesting. Although there is little work, there are food and bed for all who come, provided by the village banker out of funds placed at his disposal.

As the evening progresses the crowds begin to thin out and farmers turn their well-stocked cars homeward. The radio ceases to blare forth its programs; the sound of laughter is heard no more on the village streets; the lights go out one by one in the white houses, and quiet and peace descend upon the town. The leaves rustling in the ever-present breeze and the constant chorus arising from the deep throats of the bull-frogs and the whirring wings of the insects of the fields alone break the deep stillness of the night. Surrounded by the fertile fields which give it life, Milligan lies sleeping. A mile away in the cemetery on the hill sleep those whose toil-worn hands built in their lifetime a community of men out of a raw and unbroken prairie. Some of the memories which cluster about it are soon to die as the pioneers who still live, one by one, join their friends who have gone before. The transplanted Bohemia which the pioneers carried to the new world is disappearing slowly as the control of the community is taken over by the new generations born on American soil. New ideals and new attitudes are replacing the old, which

---

[1] That parking is a problem in Milligan is shown by the following article in the *Nebraska Signal*, July 3, 1930, p. 3:

"Where in the world do the crowds come from? Saturday night the streets were so filled with cars there was hardly a place to park. A farmer living not so far from town remarked that the nearest parking space he could find was in his own garage. He said hereafter he would save time and save gas and save his disposition by leaving the car at home and walking to town. The crowd lingers long into the night, until eleven o'clock and later. A program of good music is being arranged for the amplifier for next Saturday night and enough of this to keep the crowd entertained until midnight."

were developed in other ages while the dead were living under the oppressive rule of a Hapsburg regime. All of the old will not be lost, but rather will old and new be mingled to form a new synthesis.

The dead who sleep under the star-lit heavens and the living who rest from their daily toil in the quiet houses scattered over the darkened landscape have each played a part in building the Milligan community. An analysis of the parts that each played and a portrayal of the way in which old and new are intermingled in the social life of the community are the objectives of this book.

CHAPTER II

PEASANT PIONEERS

The earliest Czech settlers in the southeastern part of Nebraska came in the '60's, before the railroad was built. They went first to Independence, Missouri, which was as far as the trains ran at that time. There they found numbers of people who had come to seek homesteads on the great plains. Long caravans of covered wagons set off daily for the promised land. In some of these caravans were found small groups of Czechs, land-hungry peasants who were soon to secure that which they prized above everything else in the world, the soil.

The wild prairie which the pioneers found waiting for them represented the end of the trail, but the beginning was to be found in the Bohemia which they had forsaken forever. What were the social conditions which caused the migration, and what were the motives which caused men and women to break the social relationships which gave them life and urged them to go forth to build a new society on foreign soil?

Background of Czech Migration to America

All migrations are of two sorts, mass migrations whereby a whole people leave one region for another, such as the migrations of the Germanic people which occurred when the Roman Empire was crumbling, and selective migrations, whereby certain individuals or groups from within a people set out to establish a home on alien soil, such as those which occurred in the days of ancient Greece or in the settlement of the new world. Two factors are primarily responsible for the first type of migration, changes in geographical conditions within the regions occupied by the people and the plunder to be gained from the conquest of a richer nation. In the other type, migration is caused by insufficient economic opportunity for an expanding population, or a social system which prevents some groups from developing potentialities and pursuing their own way of life. Such oppression was a factor in the sailing of the Mayflower.

Migration of the Czech people to the United States comes under the second head, and one cause is to be found in the social system prevailing in Bohemia during the nineteenth century. At the Battle of White Mountain in 1620, Bohemia lost its independence, and for three centuries its inhabitants lived under the dominant and oppressive Hapsburg regime.

The liberties of the people were curtailed, and an attempt was made to Germanize the population. The nineteenth century saw a rebirth of Bohemia and the beginning of the struggle which culminated in the attainment of independence in 1918.

To the Czechs of the nineteenth century Bohemia was a land of great natural beauty, with forests and mountains, rivers and plains, and it had traditions of better days and great glories achieved in the past, during the times of Charles IV and Master Jan Hus. A consciousness of greatness in the past may feed the spirit, but glorious traditions produce little bread. All who were born in Bohemia sing of the beauty of the Czech homelands, but of what value is the generosity or the beauty of nature if most of her fruits go to feed alien bodies or to delight other souls? Under the social system of the day the German nobility owned most of the best land and the great mass of the people were condemned to a life full of hard work and little material or spiritual reward. Some of the Czechs were able to secure good land and live a life of comparative ease and comfort, but for the majority there was no such hope. When to an insufficiency of bread there are added limitations upon the life of the mind and of the spirit, an intolerable situation is created from which the human being will escape if escape is possible.

There were two ways out of the situation—migration or the creation of an independent Bohemia. Most of those who met the situation by migrating from Bohemia were peasants who lived in the small towns and villages. "A peasant is something quite distinct from anything that we know in America. On the one hand he is a link in a chain of family inheritance and tradition that may run back for centuries, with a name, a posterity, and a reputation. On the other hand, he is confessedly and consciously an inferior. It is part of his world that there should be a God in heaven, and masters (Herrenschaften, Pani) on the earth."[1] In Bohemia there were three types of peasants, the "sedlák" (farmer), who usually owned from twenty-five to one hundred acres of land and a comfortable farmhouse; the "chalupník" (cottager), who owned five to twenty-five acres of land and lived in a small cottage; and the "nádeníci" (day-laborers), who owned no land and lived in a tiny cottage on the farm of a "sedlák" or noble, for whom they worked.

A large majority of the immigrants to America came from the "chalupník," or cottager class. "The 'sedlák' was too comfortably fixed to want to leave his homeland, while the day-laborer was too poor even to think of emigrating. But

---

[1] Emily G. Balch, *Our Slavic Fellow-Citizens* (New York, 1910), p. 42.

the cottager was in a position where it was very difficult for him to make a decent living, while at the same time he was in possession of some property which could be sold or given in security in order to raise money necessary for the journey. These cottagers were steady, solid folk, possessed at least of a common-school education, and with an uncanny ability to make crops grow where an American would not dream even of attempting it. Those who left for America did so because they were anxious to forge ahead. This opportunity was denied them in Austria, and they came here to find it."[2]

Some of the immigrants had learned trades in the small towns or villages in which they lived, and came to America with some industrial experience. During the period when the Czechs were emigrating to America there was also in progress a movement from the country to the rapidly growing industrial centers of Bohemia. This migration stopped there, as almost none of the inhabitants of these centers emigrated to America.

The villages in which the peasants lived were often one long street with houses on either side. Each morning the men went from the village to their farms to work in the fields. The isolated farmhouse of America did not exist in Bohemia. In the village everyone knew everyone else, and there developed a strong feeling of community. The life of the peasant was an open book to his neighbors. His behavior was regulated by the public opinion of the community. He lived in a primary social group, and the social relationships which he formed were very close, strong, permanent, and deep. The life of the group touched all phases of his own life. In the evening the men of the village gathered at the town tavern to discuss the events of the day; the women met in the homes to strip goose feathers and gossip; the children played together on the village streets. On Sunday the men and women put on their best clothes, often dressing in the costume worn in their section of the country, and went to church to render thanks to God for His mercy. After church they strolled up and down the street, proudly displaying their costumes and receiving the greetings of their friends.

Those who left the community to come to Nebraska left life itself behind them when they set out. Away from their own village their identities were lost as they entered a strange world. It took resolution and courage to break the ties which bound them so closely to their village, and it would have been

---

[2] Kenneth D. Miller, *The Czecho-Slovaks in America* (New York, 1922), pp. 22, 23.

impossible for them to have done so unless they hoped for great gains in the new world.

Why They Came to Milligan

Poverty and large families in Bohemia were the reasons for migration given by 92 of 117 immigrants still living in Milligan.[3] It would thus appear that economic motives were mainly responsible for their emigration. Three felt that they could not endure any longer to live under the political rule of the Hapsburgs. Two did not like the fact that they were compelled to worship in Catholic Churches. Five left Bohemia late in the nineteenth century to escape military service. The other 15 came to join friends or relatives or because of wanderlust.

In a highly stratified society such as existed in Bohemia it was very difficult for a person to better himself. If he were born a day-laborer, it was almost impossible for him to become a "sedlák." It was difficult for the sons of "sedláci" to secure farms of their own. The eldest son inherited whatever property there was at the time of the death of the parents. Girls could not hope to marry successfully unless the dowry was adequate to attract desirable suitors. Thus although poverty and large families were the factors which appeared to motivate behavior, they were in turn the resultants of the social system.[4]

A better understanding of the causes of migration will be secured if the replies of individual immigrants are known.

"There were eight children in the family. My father was poor. No dowry. I saw how a poor woman had to work. I came with my brother."

"My husband was that way. He would have traveled over the whole world. He heard of America from friends' letters."

"I wanted to see how America was. I had the wanderlust. I wandered all about Europe. I heard times were good here, although one had to work. I could work hard. I was a blacksmith here, and made good money."

"I was not satisfied that I could go to school in Bohemia. My mother wanted me to become a seamstress, and I wanted to be a teacher. My folks could not send me to school, so I came to America."

[3] Eleven of 140 first-generation immigrants selected as a sample (see Introduction) could not give a satisfactory answer to why they had left Bohemia, as most of them were very young at the time. Care was taken not to duplicate the reason for migration in the case of brothers and sisters brought over in infancy. This correction reduces the number of separate reasons to 117.

[4] In this connection see Census Monograph No. VII, *Immigrants and Their Children* (Washington, 1927), p. 111.

"I had no reason. When I was very small I said that I wanted to come to America. My father's sister came here with three small children. I came along to take care of them. If I had had the money I would have gone back. I was very lonesome."

"America had a big name. We thought we would have everything here without work."

"My brother came to America with his family. My wife's sister wrote her urging her to come. She really wanted the money mother had."

Some of the quotations given above also tell why the individuals came to Nebraska. The earliest settlers came because they learned that homesteads could be secured. Those who followed did so because they had friends or relatives in the state. Some typical answers follow:

"I first came to Cleveland. There I could find no work. Some friends were going to Nebraska to take up homesteads, so I went along."

"I first lived in New York City, where I learned to make cigars. Then a strike was declared, and I came to an old uncle in Milligan."

"I read in the newspapers that there were Bohemian people here."

"I lent money to some people and had to come with them to get it back. I did not get it back and had to remain here."

"I had my way paid here; then I worked out the passage after I arrived."

"It was dry in Kansas. We came here for better land. Friends from our village in Bohemia were here."

"My father went to Wisconsin in 1869, but saw nothing but trees. He did not like it there. He heard of Nebraska from friends and came here to homestead."

What They Found

When the first settlers came to Nebraska they found a prairie country which was difficult to subdue. The land was new and unused to the plow, and the work was unending. Of the land Willa Cather writes:

"It (the land) was still a wild thing that had its ugly moods; and no one knew when they were likely to come, or why. Mischance hung over it. Its Genius was unfriendly to man. . . . This land was an enigma. It was like a horse that no one knows how to break to harness, that runs wild and kicks things to pieces."[5]

[5] Willa Cather, *O Pioneers* (New York, 1913), pp. 20–22.

Droughts and grasshoppers laid waste the fields. However, the earliest settlers had in their possession the soil which they had wanted so much, and were willing to work hard and suffer any misfortune in order to keep it. The struggle with nature tested their physical strength, and the lack of community tried their souls.

The thing the settlers missed most in America was not the greater comfort of life in Bohemia, but rather the social life of the small village from which they came.

"I missed the social life of Bohemia. All are together there. We lived in large towns there; here we lived on scattered farms."

"At first I missed everything. I did housework for an American family. There was no entertainment on the farms here; there was much over there. I missed the church. Later I went with the American family. I missed the trees and beauty of nature of Bohemia. Here I lived in a sod house."

"At first I missed the music and entertainments. Here we just sat on Sunday. There we had 'zábavy' (entertainments)."

"Here the air was heavy and I tired easily. The farms were far apart and I longed for neighbors and social life. At first there were few Czechs here, and I did not like it. My mother was always lonesome. Later I became reconciled to living here."

"I missed the village and my relatives. Here the farms are far apart; in Bohemia there is a close community life."

"I missed the social life of Bohemia. People liked each other more. Here people want to get rich; then they don't think of the poor."

Gradually the forces of nature were overcome, and more and more people arrived from Bohemia. Finally all the homesteads were taken, and still people came, buying land from the railroads and from the first settlers, who were mainly Irish. In many instances whole families moved to the new world, and in others a large part of the population of a village came to America.

Present-Day Links with Bohemia

The passage of the years and the building of a community life in this country have caused the people to forget about Bohemia. The majority of the members of the first generation miss nothing in America today. When asked what they liked best in America they gave a variety of answers. For most of them the thing which pleased them best in America was the fact that here they could earn a better living. A few believed that the greater freedom and equality to be found here meant more to them than did anything else. Fewer still found in husband or wife or children the greatest happiness which had come to them.

"A man who helps himself can live better and more safely here. A poor person in Bohemia can't help himself."

"I have worked hard and have earned little, but freedom and independence here is much better."

"I am satisfied. We had a farm and property."

"I was better satisfied when Czechs arrived here and began to buy farms from Americans. We made a good living here."

"Here rich and poor are alike; there are no social classes or distinctions."

Bleak and matter-of-fact resignation is found in the answer of a widow.

"I like nothing. I always worried. My husband was sick; he died after we were married fifteen years. That was twenty-three years ago. When I got used to it I became satisfied. I knew it could not be changed."

Another widow finds something to praise, but more to blame.

"I liked beer when it was here. I do not like prohibition. What about me? I will last it out, but if I was younger, I would go at once to Bohemia. I like Milligan, the paved streets, the new hall, the school, the children."

These answers tell why they came, what they found, and what they missed. When they first came the old world was present with them and many letters were written to friends and relatives in the old world. As the years have passed this stream has dried up. Many of the people to whom the letters were first written came to live in Nebraska. Those who are old today saw broken one after another the links which bound them to the past as death took its toll of friends and relatives in Bohemia. Several of the town's inhabitants have visited Bohemia since the World War, and while there they made new friends to whom they write occasionally. One of these visitors returned to the village in which he once lived and found that no one living there now had any recollection of his family. Some of those who were born in Bohemia quit writing because all of the letters which they received from Bohemia contained many requests for money. Some typical answers follow:

"No. I used to write, but all are dead over there. I pulled several people here with letters."

"No. I don't know anyone there. The people all want money. They think there is much money here."

"Not now; I can't see. No; no relatives remain there."

"I wrote while grandmother and aunty were alive. I sent them money."

"I write about twice a year to my parents and to my brother. When I was sad I used to write often, but I don't write very often now."

Summary

About the middle of the nineteenth century, a number of Czechs began to leave a peaceful and civilized Bohemia for a new life on the wild prairies of Nebraska. They hoped to find in the new world the social and economic opportunity which was denied to them in the country of their birth. In Nebraska they suffered many hardships. Nature was unproductive at first, and the people of other nationalities were unfriendly to them. Gradually the land was conquered, and the other nationalities learned to accept the newcomers. The Czechs came in ever-increasing numbers, until finally they constituted about ninety per cent of those living in the community.

While the struggles with nature and with other nationalities were severe, the most difficult adjustment was that which took place in the inner rather than to the outer world. In Bohemia the people had passed their lives in the close and intimate contacts of a peasant village; in America they were forced to live on isolated farms. When they first came they looked back with longing eyes at the social relationships which had made life worth while. Gradually, however, they succeeded in building a new community on the soil of Nebraska, and their lives became once more full of close and intimate social relationships. This new community which they created more nearly fulfilled their needs and desires than did that from which they had come. The memories of the old world became dim with the years. Most of the friends which the early settlers left in Bohemia have died off, and today there are few letters sent to the old world. The new world rewarded well the labor of the immigrants. Today few of them would like to return to Bohemia. They have found the economic and social opportunity which they sought, and they are content.

CHAPTER III

NEW ECONOMICS FOR OLD

Prior to 1887 the land on which Milligan now stands was used for farming. Here and there a blacksmith or harness maker took care of the work associated with these crafts, but for the most part all of the people tilled the soil. Those who came from Bohemia were confronted with a different method of cultivation, but the work was essentially of the same character as that in which they engaged in their homeland.

Occupations of Immigrant Class in Bohemia

Fathers of the immigrants now living in Milligan engaged in a number of occupations in Bohemia.[1] Four out of ten of them owned or rented a small farm. Some of these no doubt had farms which were large enough to support their families, but it is highly probable that most of them eked out their living by working as farm laborers. About one in ten of the fathers secured all of their income, such as it was, by working as farm laborers. Five out of ten secured the major portion of their livelihood by working at some trade. In most instances these individuals had some land which they farmed in addition to their craft. The trade most frequently followed by members of this group was that of mason. The next most frequently followed was that of coal mining. The others included such jobs as the following: harness maker, miller, brickmaker, tailor, mechanic, factory worker, watchman in forest, foreman, shoemaker, musical-instrument maker, manager of estate, postman, locksmith, blacksmith, coachman, woodcutter, contractor and builder, servant on estate of noble, charcoal maker, cloth-painter, basket maker, trucking. Most of these trades are associated with a simple village economy, and yielded at best a meager livelihood.

Agricultural Economy in Nebraska

Most of those who had learned crafts in Bohemia found them of little use in the new environment. Those who could use their trades, such as the blacksmiths and the harness makers, found that they had an advantage over the other settlers. One such, who set up a blacksmith shop on his

---

[1] In obtaining this data care was taken not to include duplicate information from brothers and sisters about the occupation of the same father. Answers were obtained from all 140 immigrants in sample (see Introduction), as to 128 fathers.

farm, was able from his two occupations to accumulate enough money to give each of his seven children ten thousand dollars, and still have left sufficient on which to live in his old age.

When immigrants from Bohemia settled on farms they thus found themselves living in an economy in which there was less differentiation of occupation than in their native country.   The adjustments that had to be made differed greatly, therefore, from those faced by immigrants to American cities.   In the cities the Czech peasant found a society much more highly differentiated than that from which he came, and he learned to specialize.   To some extent the trades which he learned in Bohemia were of value to him in making the adjustment.   It was relatively easy for him to learn the simple tasks required in factory employment.   Wages were ample for a life of comparative comfort.   In a sense the transition through which he passed in adjusting himself to city life was much greater than that through which the farm immigrant passed; the stresses and strains were greater, but the immediate material reward was greater, too.   If the economic adjustment was often easier, the social adjustment was usually more difficult.

Frequently the immigrant on the farm found it necessary to learn a new method of cultivation.   The small farms of Bohemia were easily cultivated by the entire family.   Labor was plentiful, and agricultural machinery not greatly needed. The larger farms of Nebraska required more capital to operate, and produced products other than those raised in Bohemia.   The soil was new to the plow, and droughts and insect pests laid waste the fields.   The pioneer's hardships were many, and he had to overcome them by his own unaided efforts.

Immigrants to Milligan before 1900 found it easier to secure land than did those coming from 1900 to 1915, when immigration from Bohemia practically ceased.   About half of the first-generation farmers of today are tenants, whereas nearly all the second-generation farmers are farm owners. The later immigrants to the Milligan district found the land all taken and selling at a high price, and were forced to rent farms from the earlier settlers who retired.   Second-generation farmers inherited farms from their parents or received them as gifts upon reaching maturity.   Living in Milligan are twenty-nine members of the first generation who have retired.   Most of these formerly tilled land which they now rent to others.

Women who live on the farms engage almost exclusively in the work of the home. Nearly all of those who have passed the age of twenty-one are married. A few unmarried still live with parents, doing housework for the family and waiting the day when they will have a home of their own. None of the members of this group have any other employment. Among those who are under the age of twenty-one, only one is married. A few are teaching school, all in one-room country schools nearby. The others attend school or college.

Occupations in Milligan Village

When Milligan was established in 1887, the economic life of the community became increasingly complex. The differentiation of occupations, however, was not like that which had obtained in the villages of Bohemia. There, production furnished the basis of differentiation; here, distribution. In Bohemia none of the fathers of the immigrants had engaged in retail trade; in the newly settled town of Milligan storekeepers arose to supply the people with the goods they needed. A few of these middlemen help the farmer to market his crops, but most of them confine their activities to getting articles to the farmers.

The professions are represented by a doctor, a dentist, a priest, and several school teachers. The first was born in Bohemia but educated in America; the next two are Czechs born in this country. A number of business men[2] employ clerks and bookkeepers; other individuals work as carpenters, barbers, pharmacists, butchers, garage mechanics, stock buyers, flour-mill operatives, blacksmiths, shoe repairers, section workers, telegraphers, telephone operators, masons, musicians, farm laborers, contractors and builders, postal employees, lumber-yard workers, managers of business establishments, practical nurses, truckmen, taxicab drivers, and highway employees.

Individuals born in Bohemia built the community, and several of them are still actively engaged in business. This condition meets with the disapproval of the American-born. These feel that the foreign-born, who are considerably older, should retire and give them a chance. They believe that the foreign-born are too old and too conservative, and that they interfere with the progress of Milligan.

One result of the tenacious hold of these elders and the limited economic opportunities in Milligan is that the more

---

[2] A list of the business establishments is given in the Introduction.

energetic and ambitious among the younger are forced to leave Milligan if they wish to get ahead in the world.[3] Some few of them do remain and go into business where they usually make a success and tread upon the toes of the elders. But there is not room for all and many young people leave for the larger cities. When one of these who had gone to New York for work was asked if he regretted leaving Milligan and would like to return, he replied:

"I like Milligan, and like to live there, but I would have no chance. The old people control everything, and I would not amount to much. I would get somewhere only after the old died off. Here in New York I am a small frog in a big puddle; in Milligan I would be a small frog in a small puddle. Here, at any rate, the puddle is. bigger and more interesting."

As a result of this selective process, it is but natural to find a larger proportion of unskilled laborers among the younger American-born Czechs. These find jobs on the farms and on the railroad. Members of the second generation have a monopoly of the positions of business manager. Five of them manage businesses varying from grain elevators to creameries. In most cases they are local managers for some corporation whose headquarters are located in a larger town.

Most of the non-Czechs who live in Milligan came to the village after they were grown and working at some occupation. In some cases they were sent to Milligan by a large corporation, such as the railroad. Some possessed sufficient capital to buy a place of business in Milligan. In other cases they possessed specialized training in education. A few non-Czechs are shiftless individuals who are employed at unskilled labor.

Three non-Czechs own business establishments in Milligan; one the lumber yard, a second the drug store, and a third one of the restaurants. The owner of the lumber yard has been in Milligan for more than a quarter of a century, while the other two business men have come but recently to the village. The drug-store proprietor is the son of a doctor who lives in a neighboring town, and has given Milligan a first-class pharmacy. Three of the non-Czechs are employed by the railroad; two at the station and one as section boss. One owns a barber shop, another works in his father's restaurant. Four are employed at unskilled labor, working for the most part on the section. One is the superintendent of schools, while the other professional worker is the Smith-Hughes (vocational) instructor and coach at the high school.

[3] This condition is responsible for the fact that so large a proportion of the population of Milligan consists of children and old people. Such an age distribution is generally found in agricultural villages in America. Cf. Luthur Fry, *American Villagers* (New York, 1926).

Finally, there is a younger man, the only one of the group born and brought up in Milligan, who works at the village drug store. He would like to leave Milligan, but has not yet been able to secure a city job.

Nearly all of these individuals have come to Milligan to get a job or to make money in business, and this is almost the only bond which holds them. If a better job or more money were to be secured elsewhere they would leave without hesitation. Only the barber and the owner of the lumber yard have lived in Milligan for a long time, and have really taken root in the life of the village.

There is one other occupation found in Milligan. The village is said to have two bootleggers, one of whom engages in his occupation quite openly and has often fallen foul of the law. The other bootlegger classifies himself as a "retired farmer," and is very careful in the selection of his clientele. Both of these men are Czechs, but the former employs one of the non-Czechs in the town as delivery man for his wares. The activities of the first bootlegger are bitterly resented by most of the inhabitants of the village, but thus far he has managed to escape a long prison term.

Czechs are a beer-drinking people and do not approve of whiskey drinkers from other towns who often enliven the Saturday night dance. Little of the profits of the bootlegging are spent in Milligan.

In the overwhelming majority of cases the place of the woman is still in the home, but some few in the community have managed to find work for which they are paid. The opportunities are limited, however, and in the case of the young women even more than in that of the young men it is necessary to leave the community in order to find a job.

The smallest proportion of full-time workers among the women is found among the members of the first generation. Of a total of forty-four only two, one widow who owns a restaurant and a middle-aged single lady who is the assistant cashier of the bank, are employed full time. One other foreign-born housewife helps her husband at certain hours in the day with his meat market. Foreign-born widows in all except one case inherited at the death of their husbands money enough to satisfy their needs.

Of twenty-nine second-generation women in the age group forty and over, two are widows who eke out a bare living by taking in washing, and one is the owner of the town hotel. In this same group are three women who have never married. Two live with parents and do housework, while one is the postmistress of the village. One wife does part-time work in her husband's store.

Nine of the thirty second-generation women between the ages of twenty-one and thirty-nine are engaged in full-time work. Six of these are teachers, one clerks in a store, one is a nurse, and the other is a telephone operator. All of these are young, and no doubt hope to marry some day. In addition four of the women clerk in stores part-time.

The trend toward employment of women in productive work outside the home is indicative of certain social trends. In Bohemia women often worked in the fields with the men, and those among the housewives who help their husbands in their stores are simply doing in another way what their women ancestors did in Bohemia. The community would frown upon the first type of activity today while it commends the other. In this instance the community has adopted the attitude of its American neighbors. Indeed, the men of the community are especially sensitive to the question of women working in the fields today, and try their best to live down the reputation which they formerly had for permitting this form of co-operation.

While women who help their husbands in the stores are repeating in a sense the experience of their grandmothers, they are not repeating it exactly. For the relationship which is established is not the same as that which existed in the earlier instance. Women could not expect to excel men as farmers; if for no other reason, because they did not possess the physical strength. Thus in such a relationship the man was the dominant member of partnership, and the woman did his bidding. However, in business the woman is often more successful than the man, and the partnership which is established is on a basis of equality. Indeed, in at least one case found in Milligan the woman has assumed the direction of the business, and the man carries out the orders which she gives.

Working wives thus have their effect on the social life of the community, as do working girls who are not married. A number of Milligan girls have gone to cities to work in offices. Few indeed go to cities to work in factories. If they are of the type for which factory work alone is possible, they usually find work as hired girls somewhere near Milligan.[4] At present two occupations are proving especially attractive to Milligan girls, teaching and nursing. Those who

[4] In this connection it is interesting to point out that the wages earned by these hired girls were often used to pay off the mortgage on the farm. Cf. Willa Cather, *My Antonia* (Boston, 1923). In this way the Czech was able to prosper while his American or Irish neighbor, who refused to permit his daughter to work out, failed to keep his farm.

learn nursing in distant hospitals seldom return to Milligan. If they return at all they return to marry someone in the community. Teaching is perhaps the profession which is most attractive. A girl does not need to go a great distance from Milligan if she wishes to teach in a country school. The local high school offers a teacher-training course, and the number of positions in Milligan and the surrounding country is large enough to provide for most of the girls who desire to teach. Their first job is in a one-room school, where they teach all grades. By taking courses during the summer in the State University they prepare themselves for more responsible positions in consolidated schools. Some of them eventually finish the normal course at the university, and seek positions in high schools. When this time comes they usually leave Milligan and find a position in one of the other towns in the state. Some of them succeed in teaching in the local high school, but many prefer to teach in some other town or city.

Among the non-Czech women in Milligan, there was but one who was engaged in productive work outside the home. She was in charge of the telephone office. One other, the daughter of the druggist, assisted her father in his store a few hours a day. However, most of the non-Czechs living in Milligan were engaged in work in which their wives could not help them. Again, nearly all of them either had no children, or had children who were still very young. When the girls of these households grow up they will no doubt engage in paid work in the community or elsewhere.

As far as labor is concerned, then, the early inhabitants of Milligan came from a simple village economy in which there was some occupational specialization based on production to a rural community in which there was almost no differentiation of occupation. The specialization which developed in Milligan was partly on the basis of production and partly on the basis of distribution. In either case the differentiation consisted of the rise of functional middlemen. It is these who have been most successful in acquiring wealth, and who control the life of the community.

Mail-Order House Competition

The Czechs are rather clannish people, and when a non-Czech is in competition with a Czech they tend to favor the latter. However, the interest of the people in economy asserts itself, and if a non-Czech gives better service at a lower cost, they buy from him rather than from one of their own number. Indeed they are even willing to buy from mail-order houses, if by so doing they are able to get good articles at a low price. This tendency is resisted by the local business men, Czech and non-Czech alike. Occasionally the newspaper runs articles such as the following:

"A great many people in this day look upon Milligan as a Bohemian town. As a matter of fact, however, Milligan is neither an Irish town nor a Scot town nor a Bohemian town, but it is a Farmers' Town. The farmers built it. And the farmers thus having put the breath of life into the thing, it certainly would be an unkindly act for them to strangle it to death. The farmers who are ashamed of their own handiwork probably have a deeper interest in building up Chicago or Kansas City, but taken as a whole, our farmers have been loyal to their offspring and apparently come to Milligan with the feeling that whatever helps Milligan as a community center helps the entire community as well."[5]

When mail-order catalogues arrive an article like the following often appears in the newspaper:

"This is the catalogue month. They pass through the country by the carloads leaving a big share of their load in country towns, where they seem to find more favorites. Montgomery Ward thought of its Milligan friends this week and unloaded a fourth ton of its advertising matter of the catalogue kind. Sears, Roebuck & Company, always very thoughtful about their interests, beat Montgomery Ward's time by several days. Next in line will be the 'National' and 'Phillipsborn' and so on down the line for probably more than twenty-five varieties. Some people use catalogues for little children to play with or cut out pictures from. Ladies use them for ideas on style, and still others use them as a source of information as to prices and names of articles, etc.; but be it as it will, to some people a mail-order catalogue remains a joke, and they would consider it an insult to the local business man to be seen with one under the arm."[6]

Hours of Work

In an industrial society it is usually customary for those who have the greater income to work fewer hours than do those whose income is small.[7] Such is not the case in Milligan. There is no correlation between wealth and hours of work, or between age and hours of work. The owner works side by side with his clerk, and often works longer in the course of a day than does his assistant. The length of the average working day in Milligan would be somewhere between ten and twelve hours. The professional men have the shortest working day, the owners of business establishments the longest. Those who work for the railroad have an eight-hour day, while telephone operators have their working time fixed at nine hours.

[5] *Milligan Times*, November 4, 1919, p. 1.
[6] *Nebraska Signal*, August 9, 1923, p. 5.
[7] Cf. R. S. and H. M. Lynd, *Middletown* (New York, 1929), Chapter VII.

When an inhabitant of Milligan says that he works twelve or fourteen, or in some cases, sixteen hours a day, he means that this much time is spent at the place in which he is employed. During open nights the clerk in the stores works at top speed to supply the customers with the things they wish to buy, but during long periods of the daylight hours he may sit around and gossip with friends who have dropped in to see him. Business men in America are reputed to allow their business to encroach upon their hours of leisure, whereas in Milligan they allow their hours of leisure to encroach upon their business.

In a system such as found in Milligan a clerk is not only a clerk, but a friend of long standing whom one meets in all of the many activities of life, and all the relationships of the past are present when one buys something from him at the store.

Home Ownership

All of the aspects of the economic life of Milligan cannot be considered, but there is one other which illustrates both persistence and change. In the old world some of the immigrants owned their home and a small piece of land. Whether this was true or not, all who came to America looked forward with eager anticipation to the time when they would be able to call some part of the new country their very own. When asked what they would like to have that they did not have now, nearly all the Czechs who live in rented quarters replied, "A home of my own." The desire to own a home is perhaps characteristic of those who live in the country; it establishes them as permanent members of the community. The Czech in Milligan who owns his own home does not feel it is his until it is free of all encumbrances. Out of ninety-nine village homes in which Czechs lived, only five were mortgaged. All of those who lived in homes with mortgages wanted to pay off the mortgage as soon as possible. Most of the twelve who lived in rented quarters had some money saved, but would not consider building a home until they had enough money to pay for it in full.

A much larger proportion of second-generation Czechs rent their homes than do first-generation members. This is due in large part to the fact that nearly all of the members of the first generation are forty years of age and over. Young people of the second generation do not have the money to buy a home when they first marry, but nearly all of them intend to have a home of their own as soon as possible. In some cases they will inherit homes from the parents when they die off. There exists in Milligan a considerable housing shortage, and the houses that are available for renting purposes are usually the least desirable in the community. This shortage is due partly to the fact that there are so many retired farmers in Milligan. Eighteen of the homes in which Czechs lived are occupied by one person, often a widow or a widower. In a number of instances the widow or widower expressed a desire to remarry. If a number of them did so, it would release some of the houses to those who wished to rent more desirable quarters. As one wag expressed it, "What Milligan needs is a good marriage broker." In Bohemia it would not have been difficult to have found such a person.

Czechs living on the farms are more likely to have mortgages on their land than are those who live in the village. The farmer is more willing to borrow money on his land, for he expects to use it for productive purposes. He is just as anxious to pay off his mortgage as is the town dweller, however.

Non-Czechs who live in Milligan are likely to be but temporary inhabitants, and one should expect to find a large proportion renting homes. Six of them rent their homes and three own them. None of the three homes owned by non-Czechs is mortgaged. Non-Czech farmers are usually permanent settlers; twice as many own their farms as rent them. Only one of the four farms owned is mortgaged.

Home ownership and freedom from debt in respect to permanent possessions are peasant characteristics which have survived in the Milligan community. The latter characteristic did not last long among Czechs who settled in cities in the new world. In Chicago, Czechs were quite willing to borrow money to build houses, and the building and loan association developed great strength. Thus in a city environment the Czechs used a means to achieve their end which is condemned by the culture represented in Milligan.[8]

When the Czechs came to Milligan they were averse to borrowing money for unproductive purposes, and they still refuse to borrow for the more permanent things of life. However, when it comes to buying commodities which are quickly consumed, they have forsaken the old folkways and do not hesitate to buy on credit. When asked what changes ought to be made in Milligan, several of the inhabitants connected with business replied, "Everything ought to be placed on a

---

[8] Cf. Jakub Horak, *The Assimilation of Czechs in Chicago* (unpublished Ph. D. dissertation, University of Chicago), p. 74.

cash basis." Here a clash between old and new world attitudes has been settled in favor of the new world.

The Chamber of Commerce

A chamber of commerce was organized in Milligan, April 23, 1924. Since its organization it has been very active in promoting business and other activities in the community. Within a few months after its organization it had demonstrated its value to the satisfaction of the local reporter.

"Since the organization of the Chamber of Commerce a number of projects beneficial to the community have been launched and enough of them carried to a successful conclusion to demonstrate the value of such an organization.

"Here are some of the things that have been accomplished during the short time that organization has been in existence: Under its auspices, the Czechoslovak band was secured to come here and give a concert. People from a distance of fifty miles and more came here to hear them and complimented the spirit of the town in having secured this truly wonderful organization. The purebred sire train committee was induced to come here for the purpose of looking us over and left with the conviction that folks here do things on a big scale and broadcast the story that there was more interest manifest in the enterprise here than at any other point where they visited. The purebred sire train is coming, too, there is no doubt about that.

"Took initial steps to put the old school ground in condition to be used as a tourist park. When the federal road is opened east of Wilber, there will be need of such a park here, and ours will be ready by that time. Called attention of the town board to the necessity of replacing some broken fire hydrants. New ones are already in place. Arranged for a meeting with the town board for the purpose of discussing the proposition of graveling the streets. There is money on hand which is to be used for the purpose of repairing the streets and alleys and without doubt it will be possible to agree with the board on some program whereby this money can be used to the best advantage.

"Monday night six laborers came to town looking for places to work in the harvest field. The committee on community co-operation called up all the farm lines to notify the farmers that this help was available, and those in need of harvest hands came and got their men. Projects are now in process of crystallization which will mean much to the town and community as a whole. There is no use talking, there is no limit to which a community may build and grow if it just has the proper spirit and willingness to co-operate for the promotion of the good of the whole."[9]

In most communities the state determines which holidays shall be celebrated, and how they are to be celebrated. In Milligan the Chamber of Commerce soon took it upon itself to make decisions with respect to holidays.

"The matter of observances of holidays was another subject much discussed and finally a tentative plan agreed upon. Six holidays are

[9] *Nebraska Signal*, July 3, 1924, p. 5.

to be observed, and on these days the business men will be asked to close from noon until 6 o'clock in the evenings. Following are the days: New Year's, Christmas, Memorial, Independence, Armistice, and Thanksgiving.

"Further it was decided to do some sort of decorating during the holiday season. Two large Christmas trees will likely be set up at the intersection of Main Street. The school will give a Christmas program and the children's treat on Tuesday, the twenty-second.

"Finally, a suggestion which met with general approval was that we celebrate the Fourth of July. It seems a little early to talk about the Fourth of July before Christmas, but it's well enough to plan far enough ahead to do something worth while, and so from now on this matter will be in mind and something big will likely be pulled off when the proper time comes."[10]

When boosters meet boosters the sky is the limit. Such an event occurred during the spring of 1930.

"Word has been received here from the Omaha Chamber of Commerce that a train load of 100 business men from Omaha will visit Milligan on a 'good will trip' Thursday, May 22, from 5:40 to 6:05. One of Omaha's best bands will accompany the party, and they are bringing with them two cars of souvenirs for distribution.

"The Milligan Chamber of Commerce will make arrangements to greet the visitors and will make an effort to impress upon them the fact that Milligan is a lively burg which measures up to Omaha standards in everything but size and what it lacks in size it makes up in quality.

"This will be the first visit Milligan has enjoyed of this nature. This is due largely to the fact that we are off the usual beaten paths of commerce and travel, but when once we've been located most of our visitors seem to have no trouble in remembering that we're here."[11]

Milligan with its Chamber of Commerce is a far cry from the villages and small towns of the Bohemia of the last century. Here again is noted a change in the attitudes of the people. In Milligan there is an insistent emphasis on the idea of progress. In Bohemia the people were generally content with what they had, and where they were not content they did not believe conditions could be changed. In Milligan the Chamber of Commerce is never satisfied with conditions as they are, but is always trying to "improve" the town. It is the real power back of all the changes which go on. It is constantly trying to do big things in a big way, and helps the townspeople to compensate for any feelings of inferiority which they may have because of the smallness of the town. Whatever inferiority feeling there is is due to the size of the town, and not to the composition of the inhabitants.

[10] *Nebraska Signal*, November 26, 1925, p. 5.
[11] *Nebraska Signal*, May 8, 1930, p. 5.

Summary

The immigrants came from a more differentiated economy into a simple farming frontier. Of the many craftsmen among the Bohemian pioneers only the harness maker and black-smith could ply their trade in the community fifty years ago. A differentiation of labor based chiefly on distribution has since sprung up in Milligan, but the chief occupation is still farming. About two-thirds of the farmers own their land. Five-sixths of the families in the town own their homes and only five per cent of these are mortgaged. The usual small businesses exist in Milligan and are to some extent still con-trolled by members of the first generation. The mail-order houses give the local stores keen competition. There is not much opportunity in Milligan for young people to find em-ployment and many of them go to the cities to work. The married women mostly work in their own homes. A few widows are gainfully employed, and the young girls as a rule take up teaching or nursing. Most of them marry early, how-ever. The Chamber of Commerce was organized in 1924 and has given valuable leadership to the business interests of the town.

CHAPTER IV

BOHEMIANS AND THE BALLOT

The Town Board Meeting

On a side street close by the new auditorium stands a garage-like building in which the government of Milligan centers. The front part of the lower floor contains a workshop and the village fire equipment. Above is the room in which voters register their preference on election days, and where the town trustees meet once a month to direct the political destinies of the village. In the center of this room is an old desk, in which the village records are kept.

On a hot night in July the five members of the village board are seated about the desk. The chairman, and the unofficial "Mayor" of the town, is the manager of one of the local grain elevators. The clerk of the board and another of the members present help their fathers manage business establishments in Milligan. The village banker and a retired farmer complete the board. No one wears a coat, and only the banker has on a collar and tie.

Routine matters are disposed of, and then the city fathers take up the important business of the evening, the resignation of the town marshal. The town marshal is not only the town marshal; he is also the "water commissioner" in charge of the town pumps; he paints the parking lines on the village streets; and he cares for all miscellaneous tasks connected with public order. In the past the position went of right to the head of the poorest and largest family in town—thus, in one measure, providing for both the poor relief and the public order of Milligan. But while this appointment solved one difficulty it created others, and the board had finally changed its policy in the selection of the present incumbent, who was chosen because of his fitness.

Jim, the town marshal, soon appears and tenders his resignation in person. He gives as his reason that his wife objects to the long hours the job requires. This is not the true cause of the difficulty. All present are aware of the real trouble, but it takes much diplomatic handling on the part of the banker, Charlie, to elicit from Jim that he resents some critical remarks Charlie had made about him one day in the store. Then Charlie assures him that he is thoroughly satisfied with his work and always has been.

After a considerable discussion, it is finally decided that Jim should hire someone to work for him whenever he thinks he needs a rest, the wages of the substitute to be paid by the village. In this fashion the situation is solved in a manner satisfactory to all concerned, and the village of Milligan is safe for another month from the danger of being without a marshal, water-tender, and handy man.

Local Politics

The town board which meets on this hot July night is one in a line of similar town boards. Nearly all of the present members had to be drafted into service. The office carries with it a great deal of responsibility, provides no financial return, takes much time, and results in but little prestige.

At one time interest in local politics was very keen; two tickets were in the field, and bitter contests occurred. Charges and countercharges flew back and forth, and every method was employed by each faction to win the elections. Sometimes the law stepped in to set limits beyond which candidates might not go in their efforts to win votes.

"The local political campaign just opening will probably be the dryest one that ever struck this vicinity, or, in fact, the county. Candidates are not allowed to set-em-up to the foaming pivo (beer), cigars, or other refreshments that will require the expenditure of money; and so ice water, cornfield handshakes, and a whole lot of talk will have to be used instead on susceptible voters. For the candidate who is possessed of a social nature and liberal disposition this will be a hardship, but for the fellow who wants your vote, but hates like thunder to even chip in for a livery rig to come to town and ask for it, it will be a God-send."[1]

The efforts of a watchful state were not always appreciated by a thirsty electorate.

Interest in state and national politics is still keen in Milligan, but the waters of the local political scene have not been troubled in many years. The apparent indifference to local political affairs has been the subject of comment on the part of other communities in the county, but the local attitude is ably defended in the following article:

"The Signal last week commented on the fact that the Milligan ballot for the village and the school board election contained the names of no candidates and left the voters free to go to the polls and write in the name of anyone whom they pleased for the places to be filled. If the Signal were as close an observer of Milligan events as it should be, it would have seen in this no casual occurrence. . . . It has probably been fifteen or twenty years since a caucus has been

[1] *Nebraska Signal*, October 13, 1899, p. 7.   Quoted from *Milligan Journal*.

held here to nominate candidates for the village officers. And the
interesting feature of it is that nothing has been lost thereby. . . .
"A village fight or a school fight may break the monotony of an
otherwise quiet life, but it does more than that. It breaks up the
spirit of co-operation without which no community can prosper or
progress. And when the fight is over, like engaging in a lawsuit, both
sides of the controversy are the losers."[2]

Although there is apparent indifference to local politics,
and although no formal caucus is held before the election,
yet the voters are not without some direction when the time
comes to elect the village trustees. A few rather able poli-
ticians in the town manage to run elections pretty much to
suit themselves, and the men whom they prefer sit on the
town or school board. One of these men, the village banker,
is the political "boss" of the village, and has been elected
three times to the State Senate on the Democratic ticket. Of
him one of the Milligan girls who attended the State University wrote as follows:

"We have one eminent man living in town, and he was a Nebraska
State Senator in 1923 and is again in 1927. He always was the outstanding character, and people all went to him for advice and help in
business and domestic affairs. He is a good speaker, and since gain-
ing recognition he has been called outside the community to deliver
graduation and political addresses, Memorial Day, and also fraternal
addresses. Years ago he was a Fillmore County School Superintendent, and also took part in the Spanish-American War and was an
officer."[3]

Much of what Milligan is today is due to the influence over
its destinies exercised by this leader of its people.

Membership in Political Parties

Of the two major political parties in the United States,
the Czechs have usually favored the Democratic, and the
Czechs in Milligan are no exception to this rule. Thus the
Catholic Irish and the anti-clerical Czechs have oddly enough
found themselves on the same side in the political arena.
Fillmore County usually gives the Republican Party a majority of its votes in county, state, and national elections, but
the townships heavily populated by Czechs almost invariably
cast Democratic votes.

When a Czech citizen of the Milligan district goes to the
polls to cast his or her ballot, the chances are about two in
three that he will vote for the Democratic ticket, about one
in ten that he will vote for the Republican Party, and about

---

[2] *Nebraska Signal*, April 13, 1922, p. 5. Article written by the Milligan Correspondent.
[3] From an unpublished manuscript entitled *Community Attitudes; A Study of a Town* (University of Nebraska, 1927).

one in six that he will "split his ticket." The chances of his
remaining at home and not voting at all, either because of
lack of citizenship or indifference, are about one in seven.
This is the situation as regards all Czech voters, male and
female.

Between the men and women there is little difference, except that many more women will remain at home and not
vote at all. Politics is still looked upon pretty much as a
man's business in Milligan. The hand that rocks the cradle
rules the kitchen, but not the ballot box.

Voting habits are given by sex and generation in Table
IV:

TABLE IV

VOTING HABITS

(Of 348 Czechs in the Milligan Community)

PARTY	First Generation			Second and Third Generations			All Generations		
	Men	Women	Both	Men	Women	Both	Men	Women	Both
Democratic	44	35	79	70	61	131	114	96	210
Republican	6	6	12	15	11	26	21	17	38
Split	12	4	16	19	23	42	31	27	58
Never Voted	6	10	16	6	20	26	12	30	42
	65	55	123	110	115	225	178	170	348

Country people are usually more conservative than city
people, and even though Milligan is but a small village, one
would expect to find some difference in respect to voting between Czechs who live in Milligan and those who live in the
country. There is more of a tendency for those who live in
the village to vote a split ticket. In the village 44 of 203 were
independent in their voting, in the country 14 of 145. This
is true in spite of the fact that the proportion of first-generation individuals is much greater in the town than it is in the
country population. There are more non-voters among the
country women than among village women. Eighteen out of
69 women in the country, and seven out of 101 village women
did not vote. The difference between men non-voters in village and country is not appreciable.

While the majority of the people who live in and about
Milligan are of Czech extraction, not all are, and the political
preferences of the non-Czech group differ distinctly from
those of the Czechs. The non-Czechs are much more apt to
be independent in their voting. If they do prefer a straight
ticket they are just as likely to vote the Republican as the
Democratic ticket. Of 43 non-Czechs, 11 were Democratic,
12 Republican, 16 Independent, and four non-voters.

If the average Czech in Milligan is asked to tell for which party he usually votes, he replies with great emphasis and apparently supreme conviction, "Demográt." If he is asked why he votes for this party, an expression of hurt surprise and annoyance appears on his face, and with considerably less conviction and with greater reluctance he gives his reason. If a non-Czech is asked these questions the English may be better, but the answer to the latter is no less obscure and unconvincing.

A few typical responses of the men and women interviewed will perhaps serve to give some understanding of the way the minds of these voters work. When asked the questions, "How do you vote?" and "Why do you vote for the Democratic (or Republican) Party?" some first-generation men were uncertain, while others believed they knew why they voted.

"Democratic. I'm too old to know why. It's just my idea; a habit now."

"Democratic. I am wet. I was a Republican, but I don't like 'Republican prosperity' and prohibition. My old friends were Republicans, but now most of them are dead."

Similar replies were given by men of the second generation.

"I vote for the Democrats. My father told me to vote Democratic."

"Democrat. I believe in that side. It's the better side. I don't know why."

"I got started voting Democratic. A friend of mine told me to vote for the Democrats. I don't know the difference between the parties."

The women of both generations leaned heavily on the men for advice.

"Democratic. My husband was a Democrat. I thought he had reason. I don't know if the other side is better."

"My father is a Democrat. My husband wanted me to vote Democràtic. I never vote unless a Bohemian is running."

In a large proportion of the cases the conclusion reached was that the individuals voted for the Democratic Party because their fathers had done so before them. A large majority of the women were influenced by either husbands or parents, with the husband being the decisive factor in quite a few more instances than were the parents.

Next after the personal influence of relatives and friends, the belief was given that the Democratic Party had the right attitude toward certain issues of the day and was the poor man's party. Both men and women favored the Democratic Party on the basis of economic issues, but many more men gave this reason than did women. Some of the men were aroused over the subject of prohibition, and expressed their intention of voting for the Democratic Party as long as it promised the return of beer and wine. A few of the men voted for the Democratic Party because they believed the Republican Party to be corrupt, and a few because they agreed with the political philosophy of the party. One of the latter mentioned the writings of Jefferson as having influenced his decision.

The scarcity of Republicans among the Czechs of Milligan made it impossible to gather much data concerning their reasons for voting. However, the replies of the Republicans did not differ greatly from those of the Democrats, except that they believed the Republican Party instead of the Democratic would bring prosperity. In the replies of both Democrats and Republicans there was displayed a lack of understanding of the positions of the parties on the issues of the day.

The reasons given by both Republicans and Democrats are summarized under very general headings in Table V:

TABLE V

REASONS FOR MEMBERSHIP IN POLITICAL PARTIES
(As given by 248 Czech Men and Women)

	Men	Women
Personal Influence	54	89
Issues	48	11

	Men	Women
Moral	6	0
Economic	35	10
Prohibition	7	1

	Men	Women
Qualifications of Candidates	5	3
Miscellaneous	16	4
No Reason	12	6
Total	135	113

Men are much more influenced by issues and miscellaneous reasons than are women. The miscellaneous reasons given are for the most part no reasons whatever, often being as follows: "It's the better side." "My party." "A habit." "Must be two sides, and I chose the Republican."

The conclusions drawn with respect to the reasons women give for voting raise the question whether these responses are typical of women in America in general, or whether these responses were due to the fact that the group is a Czech group.

This tendency is also very strong among the non-Czech women in Milligan, but this group is so small as to be of little value in a comparison of this sort. This question could be answered conclusively only if a study were made of various immigrant groups and of groups in which the members are native-born Americans. Regardless of the questions which may be raised, the results do show that Milligan men reacted in a different way to politics than did the women, and that a campaign which would win the men would probably have little effect on women except as they were influenced indirectly by their own men-folk.

Political Background

From a consideration of the answers it would appear that the Czechs in Milligan vote for political parties for much the same reasons that people generally in America do.[4] They are no more alert politically than are other Americans, in spite of the fact that they came to this country with a keen political consciousness which was developed under the conditions prevailing in Bohemia at the time they emigrated. The oppression of the Hapsburg regime had made life rather difficult for the Czechs, and the Sokol movement fostered an interest in the elimination of the abuses which existed. Autonomy within the monarchy was one of the ends proposed, while an independent Bohemia was the other. Various means were suggested to realize the ends. It became apparent that the first could not be achieved regardless of the means employed because of the treachery of the Hapsburg rulers. All efforts were directed toward the achievement of the second end. This was finally realized during the World War. During the course of this struggle the Czech people developed a great interest in politics and government.

When the Czech immigrants came to the United States they usually joined the Democratic Party. It was the minority party, and the Czechs believed that it stood for the rights of the common people as opposed to wealth and privilege. In Europe they had tried to overthrow privilege and aristocracy, and they did not want to support it here. The special conditions prevailing in Nebraska during the decades following the Civil War, when the heavy immigration of the Czechs into the state occurred, also helped to turn them toward the Democratic Party. The restless, debt-ridden West blamed the wealthy, Republican East for its woes and turned to

---

[4] "Statistical data on this point (reasons for voting) are not available, but from numerous tests we have made over a period of twenty years, the percentage of 'hereditary' voters runs from 65 per cent to 85 per cent, averaging about 75 per cent."
      Charles E. Merriam and Harold F. Gosnell, *The American Party System* (New York, 1921), p. 28.

follow other leaders, the most notable of whom was the "boy orator of the Platte," William Jennings Bryan. The Czechs of Milligan were ever interested in hearing his orations; the local newspaper often reported that the small crowd at village affairs was due to the fact that many of the inhabitants had gone to another town to listen to his magic voice.

It would appear that man today becomes interested in politics only when faced with suffering. Thus the prosperity which came to the Czech immigrants to Milligan caused them to lose their political consciousness. The seeds of their present political behavior were laid in the troubled days when the community was young. Since then voting for a particular party has become a habit, broken only when economic depression lays its heavy hand on the community.

Attitudes Toward Women's Suffrage

Women's suffrage is a relatively recent phenomenon in the history of the world. It represents part of a larger social movement, which has resulted in women achieving a new status in the social order. In most of the peasant countries of Europe the woman is still the unpaid worker in the home and the willing servant of the male. In Bohemia women occupy an inferior status as compared with men even today, although they have been given the vote and an attempt has been made to raise their position in the social order.

The attitudes of the Czechs living in Milligan toward the question of women's suffrage reflect both the old world and the new. Of 105 first- and second-generation men forty years of age and over, 47 were in favor of women's suffrage and 58 were opposed to it. The younger men in the Milligan community believe very decidedly in women's suffrage. In the age group twenty and under, 42 favored it, seven opposed; in the age group twenty-one to thirty-nine, 54 favored and 16 opposed the policy. Thus at first glance it would appear that age is more important than place of birth in determining the attitude toward women's suffrage.

This conclusion does not hold when other factors are taken into consideration. In the first place, all of the older men were brought up in a culture that was Czech rather than American. The older men of the second generation were reared on American soil, but not in American traditions. When they were young schools were few in number, the term was short, educational standards were low, and the work of the farm demanded their presence at home at an early age. Thus the home was a much more potent influence than the school in shaping their attitudes, and the home in this case was one in which the traditions of the old world were very strong. Many of the members of this group speak the Czech language much better than they do English. For the most part, they have traveled but little and their contact with the life of America has been slight. Their outlook is Czech rather than American, and when they speak on the question of women's suffrage their voice is that of the old world rather than that of old age.

When the non-Czechs are considered, additional evidence is secured that the old world is more important than age in determining the attitude toward women's suffrage. All the groups among the non-Czechs are strongly in favor of wo- men's suffrage. Only six out of 49 were opposed. Age makes some difference, but not a great deal. Even the group which includes men over forty voted nine to three in favor of women's suffrage. Better education, a different set of home traditions, a greater flexibility of customs, and a wider contact with the general life of America have combined to create a more liberal attitude toward this question. As the members of the Czech group come into contact with the same influences, their attitudes approach those of the non-Czech group. That this process has gone far among some of the Czech groups is quite evident.

Among 89 first- and second-generation Czech women forty years of age and over, 47 favor women's suffrage, 42 oppose it. In all other age groups among the women the sentiment is overwhelmingly in favor of women's suffrage. In the age group twenty-one to thirty-nine, 62 favor women's suffrage, 15 are opposed; in the age group twelve to twenty, 52 favor it, three oppose. As is perhaps to be expected, women are more strongly in favor of women's suffrage than are men. One hundred and sixty-two of 222 Czech women favored women's suffrage. The influence of the old world is present among the women, however, as among the men. The non-Czech women are much more strongly in favor of women's suffrage than are the Czech women. Only two out of 27 were opposed to it. In many of the families in which live the older Czech women, the husband is still the head of the household, and the wife follows his thought patterns. These in turn have come from the old world.

For a very large majority of the people a sufficient reason for preferring women's suffrage was that women have the same rights as men. An answer to the question on the basis of abstract rights does not tell all that the people had in their minds. Back of this question of abstract rights is, of course, the whole struggle of woman to acquire a status equal to that of man. When the people answered that women had the same right as men to vote, they really meant that woman possessed an individuality apart from that of the particular man to whom she was married, and that her personality counted for as much as that of her mate. It is this strange new notion which the old folks, whose early lives were lived in a community with different folkways and mores, find it hard to accept.

A rather strong minority of the people believed that women should vote because they are as intelligent as men, and as capable of understanding politics as are men. Some of the other reasons, which were given in each case by relatively few, were as follows: Women work, and hence are entitled to vote; more votes are cast if women vote; women obey laws, and hence are entitled to make them; women's influence is a good one; women vote for prohibition; women were far behind when men voted. Some of these answers are intelligent, but one at least appears to be a queer example of reasoning. Why it should be a desirable thing to have more votes cast at a given election it is rather difficult to see. Those who gave this answer would not let in further light.

Non-Czechs living in the Milligan district expressed a greater preference for women's suffrage than did the Czechs, but when it came to giving reasons for their attitude, the minds of the non-Czechs seemed to run in the same channel as those of the Czechs.

Some typical answers of the Czechs follow:

"Yes, they have as much right as men. Some with good education will run an office better than a man."

"Yes, it is so arranged that the women should vote, and so it must be a good thing."

"Their judgment is as sound as that of men. Their reason is as good. They can read. They have more time to devote to politics."

"Yes. Men vote for personality and not for what a person may do. Women would pay more attention to candidates' fitness."

"It makes little difference either way. As long as they are intelligent, educated people, it matters little who votes."

"I don't know. I didn't get that far in school yet."

"We are all created equal. Women should have a chance like men."

"Yes. If only men voted, there would not be as many votes. There are more votes that way."

"They can make better and cleaner laws and can enforce them better. You can't buy a woman off."

"Yes. I got used to it."

"Women should have a voice in things. They helped bring in prohibition."

During the summer in which this study was made a woman ran for one of the county offices. The feeling against her was very strong, and the community was greatly relieved when she was defeated in the primary. The community believes that political offices should be filled by men because the man supports the family. Women who take political offices away from men are taking away from them a means of livelihood.

A great variety of reasons were given for opposing women's suffrage. The one which was most frequently given by the men was that women did not understand politics, as politics is man's work, and not that of woman. Enough women agreed with the men on this point to cause this answer to receive the largest number of votes among those opposed to women's suffrage. The next popular answer among the men was that women voted for prohibition. With the temperature running up to 114 degrees in the shade, women's treachery in this respect seemed inexcusable to the men, and was sufficient justification for refusing them further use of the ballot. What was the ballot compared to beer?[5]

Some typical answers follow:

"The man is head of the house, and has the right to vote. The woman is in the back."

"I used to believe in it, but now I don't think they pay as much attention to the question of politics as they do to social interviews. They are too easily led."

"No. Woman's place is in the home, cooking dumplings and sauerkraut."

"No, there is too much swindle. Women have long hair and short reason. They don't know enough to vote. Man alone has the right to vote."

"No, I don't have that idea. Every wife does not have good ideas; she does not vote right. The world is badly off today because they voted. If the woman is widowed or single, she should vote. Wives should not vote, because they vote as their husbands do, and thus just double the work."

The answers to the question of women's suffrage represent cloudy thinking, unscientific correlations, and a multitude of other things. Most of those who gave them are old in years. The social life which produced the attitudes displayed here has passed away. Nevertheless, it is of human

---

[5] In this connection it is interesting to note that women are blamed for voting for prohibition, whereas actually the state of Nebraska adopted prohibition in 1916, several years before the women obtained the ballot.

beings whose minds work much as these do that society is composed, and social action is often based on attitudes which are arrived at much as these were.

Analysis of Changes

From the evidence submitted it has been possible to gather some conception of the way in which the minds of the people of Milligan work when confronted with a problem in the field of the social sciences. To a great extent the attitudes of the members of the community are determined for them by the folkways and mores of the community in which they spent their early years. The pioneers who came to this country in the late decades of the last century received their social inheritance to a pretty large extent through the family circle. In the early days in this country the family was primarily responsible for the development of the attitudes of the community. Thus we find but little difference between the attitudes of the older members of the first and second generations, because they received their mind-sets from a common source. As the social structure of the community became differentiated and other associations took over some of the tasks which formerly had been fulfilled by the family, we find a change occurring in the attitudes held by the members of the community. Today it is only certain isolated farm families which resist these influences. The little girl who said that she could not tell whether women's suffrage was good or bad because she had not gotten that far in school yet was pointing out the means whereby the change has been effected in the attitudes of the members of the community. The school belongs to the new country, and the social forces which are a part of the common life of America operate through the school system to break down the old Czech community of Milligan and make of the elders who built it strangers in the society which they helped to create.

CHAPTER V

CHURCHLESS CZECHS

Religious Background of Immigrants

When Bohemia lost its independence at the Battle of White Mountain in 1620, it also lost its religion. The tradition of John Hus and the Bohemian and Moravian Brethren had been very strong, especially in the country districts; the Catholic Church was very bitter against the Bohemian people and after the Austrian conquest it did all in its power to stamp out the heresy which had arisen some two centuries before. The Czechs were required to belong to the Catholic Church which was an arm of the Austrian state and which sought at all times to promote the welfare of the Hapsburg kings.

For some two centuries or more the Bohemian people lived under the oppressive rule of Church and State. When the fires of nationalism swept over Europe in the middle of the nineteenth century there awakened in the minds of many Czech patriots a desire to secure for Bohemia political independence. The movement towards autonomy was opposed by the Catholic Church as well as by the Austrian state. State and Church were really one and the political struggle which aroused hatred against the State also succeeded in developing bitter resentment against the Church.[1] As a result of this condition a large proportion of those who emigrated from Bohemia to other parts of the world during the past century have withdrawn from the Catholic Church and many of these have not allied themselves with any of the Protestant denominations.

Church Membership of Czechs in Milligan

Of 509 Czechs in the community who were asked to state their church allegiance, 359 reported that they belonged to no church; 141, that they belonged to the Catholic Church, 23 of whom attended irregularly, if at all; and nine that they belonged to the Methodist Church. Thus nearly 70 per cent of the Czech inhabitants of Milligan belong to no church and the other 30 per cent are largely Catholic. Among the first generation, 67 per cent were non-church members, while there were 73 per cent among the second generation and 71 per

---

[1] Cf. H. A. Miller, *Races Nations and Classes* (Philadelphia, 1926), Chapter 5.

cent among the third generation. There were no Methodists among the first generation, six among the second, and three among the third. Eighty-one women have retained their allegiance to the Catholic Church, as compared with 60 men.

Other studies have been made of church allegiance among Czech immigrants to America.[2] Most of them present data similar to the statistics secured in the present study. The fact that Czech immigrants do not join Protestant churches means that one of the avenues whereby their culture might be changed is missing among them. The Catholic Church is a conservative body and appeals mainly to older people who were brought up in the Catholic Church and who have resisted attempts to change their faith. The Methodist Church, to which some of the Czechs belong, has had rather a difficult time in Milligan. As one of the non-Czech farmers remarked, "They've tried to put a Protestant church in Milligan time and again but the people always drive them out. They can't support a regular minister and even the Sunday School doesn't amount to much. Milligan needs a Protestant church to teach the people how to behave."

The Catholic Church in Milligan

In spite of the fact that a very large proportion of the inhabitants of Milligan do not belong to a church, there is no great feeling of animosity toward churches. Indeed, there is at least an outward semblance of harmony. The Catholic priest in 1930 was a second-generation Czech who was greatly admired and respected by all the inhabitants of Milligan. However, the priest who preceded him in Milligan was not as well liked. He was a Belgian who tried to impress upon all the members of his congregation the necessity of adhering very strictly to a dogmatic theology. At one time he advised several of the girls of his congregation not to associate with the daughters of one of the most influential families in the village because this family believed in and supported the Methodist Church.

In his attempt to promote the interests of the Catholic Church in Milligan, the priest used the columns of the county newspaper. He resorted to this means of communication because he was not reaching all of the members of his congregation from the pulpit. He was particularly desirous of reaching the children, as the following quotations show:

"Every Saturday at 9 a. m. school of Christian doctrine for the boys and girls as well as for the children. I wish to convince parents of

[2] Cf. Edmund de S. Brunner, *Immigrant Farmers and Their Children* (New York, 1929), Chapter VI.

the great necessity of having their children, small or big, instructed in the religion of their parents and ancestors. Neglect in matters of such importance in this life and above all in the next, will bear lamentable fruits. Faith and its upbuilding must be kept in the minds of parents and be watched as the most precious treasure which Jesus died for and was crucified at the cross."[3]

"Since God made us to know Him, love Him, and serve Him in this world and to be happy with Him forever in the next, it follows, as a necessary consequence that we are bound to learn what those means are, and how to employ them. Now, we acquire this necessary knowledge by acquiring a knowledge of our religion, and, therefore, attending catechetical instruction is the chief means by which people generally come to know their religion. I will show, first, the necessity of each one learning his religion, of the obligation of attending to religious instruction; second, the great advantage of becoming well instructed; and third, the lamentable evils arising from ignorance."[4]

While the priest was greatly concerned with seeing that the children grew up in the way of the faith, he was no less interested in the education of the adult members of his congregation. In some of his communications he pointed out the obligations imposed on them by their faith.

"Don't forget that Christians do not attend dances during Lent because God calls us to penance and through it to grace and salvation."[5]

"Ember days are on September 15, 17, and 18. The church commands to fast and abstain from flesh meat on these days in order that we may mortify our passions and satisfy our sins according to the gospel."[6]

At another time the spiritual leader discussed the existence of God and of the soul.

"How do we know that there is a God? The very fact of our own existence proves it, for, if we ask ourselves this question: 'Who made me?' we can find no reasonable answer except this, 'A self-existing Being.' Again, if we ask the different things around us, their answer must be the same. From this self-existence of God all His other perfections flow. The magnificence and harmony of the creation prove it; all nature proclaims the existence of God. Conscience proves there is a God, that there is an all-seeing witness, for whence comes that pleasure which we experience after performing good works, consolation in patient suffering, confidence in death? Whence comes that remorse after secret crimes and terrors at death? Hence there cannot be a real atheist."[7]

"How do we know that the soul does not die? First, from reason. The soul is a spirit, and reason shows that it is not the nature of a spirit to die, because, being a simple, immaterial substance, it contains in itself no principle of dissolution. Second, from the divine justice. God will reward virtue and punish vice. Now it very often happens that during life the wicked prosper, etc., while the good are afflicted, oppressed, persecuted unto death, etc., but if there was no future life

³ *Nebraska Signal*, April 29, 1926, p. 5.
⁴ *Nebraska Signal*, January 27, 1927, p. 5.
⁵ *Nebraska Signal*, March 18, 1926, p. 5.
⁶ *Nebraska Signal*, September 9, 1926, p. 5.
Nebraska Signal, April 12, 1928, p. 5.

where would be the justice of God? This consideration made the psalmist say: 'Behold these are sinners, and yet abounding in the world they have obtained riches—and I have been scourged all the day—I have studied that I might know this thing; it is labor in my sight until I go into the sanctuary of God and understand concerning their last ends.' "[8]

Occasionally the priest turned his eyes to the world about him and called the attention of his congregation to the position of the church in Bohemia.

"In Czechoslovakia the Catholics and Slovaks under the leadership of Rector Hlinka, have joined with the government. If the young republic develops peace and order, much will be gained by all Europe.

"Czechoslovakia inherited the national problems of old Austria. Czechs, Slovaks, Germans, Hungarians, and Poles live under the same roof in that republic. The Czechs themselves do not represent the majority of the country, yet for eight years the Czech nationalists and socialists sought to establish a chauvinistic rule.

"All the other nationalities were excluded from the government, which meant the rule of the Hussite sectarian spirit, the infringement of the rights of the Catholic movement and perpetual religious strife. The so-called land reforms robbed the bishoprics of the larger part of their estates, supporting the charitable and scientific institutions. The archbishopric of Olmustz, the abbeys of Osseg Tepl were subjected to persecutions and threatened with bitter poverty. Church monuments, like the famous statue of St. Mary at Prague, were destroyed.

"The more, however, the two allies, Czech free-thinking and Czech socialism raged, the more unseemly became their rule. The last election resulted in so decisive a victory for the non-socialist parties that a change of system became an absolute necessity. German Catholics stretched out their hands to the Czech Catholics in a spirit of reconciliation. The Germans were admitted to the cabinet. 'Czechoslovakia can exist only as a state of nationalities, but not as a national state,' said the archbishop of Prague. Moreover he declared: 'We Czechs have no longer to fear suppression at the hands of others, therefore we must exert tolerance towards the other nationalities. The unfortunate rule of the free-thinking and socialists is at an end and a new era begins for the young state with Christian principles maintained by strong parties prevailing in the government.' "[9]

One hope of the Father was to unite the community under the banner of his Church. When the Catholic holidays came around he would appeal to the community to support the Church in its activities.

"Holy-week activities will be held at the St. Wenceslaus Church. The whole community is invited to attend these impressive services which commemorate the passion and death of our Lord Jesus."[10]

"Keep in mind the Corpus Christi bazaar to be held June 3. We want to make this year's Corpus Christi festivities the biggest ever

[8] *Nebraska Signal*, January 10, 1929, p. 5.
[9] *Nebraska Signal*, March 3, 1927, p. 5.
[10] *Nebraska Signal*, March 25, 1926, p. 5.

held in Milligan and in this undertaking we solicit the co-operation of the community."[11]

These latter appeals were generally heeded by the community, not because the Father made them, but in spite of this fact. A bazaar has always been looked upon as a community affair by the people of Milligan. All the inhabitants co-operate to make the occasion a success.

Father Verhelst remained but a relatively short time in Milligan. While he knew his religion, he did not understand his community. In the first place, his use of logic to expound Catholic doctrines did not serve to convince the people of their truth. For logic can be met with logic, and there is nothing that Czech people like better than to argue the merits of some abstract principle. Instead of removing difference, the priestly logic gave a basis for its development.

When the priest turned from logic to a categorical statement of the position of the Church, he was again on dangerous ground. The question at once arose in the minds of his readers, "How do you know that what you say is true?" The questioning character of the Czech mind which causes it to challenge logic also causes it to disagree with traditional dogmas which no good church member ever denies. Thus, instead of making converts he was whetting the appetites of the people for intellectual skirmishes with those who believed in the dogmas of the Church. Instead of holding the faithful he was forcing them into a defense of their faith.

As long as he restricted his remarks to purely theological questions, there was no great harm done. But when he chose to discuss the politics of Czechoslovakia from the viewpoint of the interest of the Catholic Church in that state, he made a fatal error. In effecting the revolution which created the Czechoslovak state in 1919, the people had been united by the bonds of patriotism even though they were divided in religion. Catholics and non-Catholics among the Czechs in America worked hard to create the new state, and believe firmly that its acts since its creation have been just. In his discussion of present political conditions in Czechoslovakia, the priest analyzed conditions from the viewpoint of the German Catholic opposition to the new government. Even his own parishioners could not swallow this, while the introduction of religion into politics served to arouse once more the old bitterness which had been felt toward the Church in pre-war Bohemia. The effect of his action was to create dissension rather than unity.

[11] *Nebraska Signal*, March 18, 1926, p. 5.

Finally, when the priest found skepticism and doubt among the members of his congregation he tried to stifle it by discouraging the faithful from associating with the non-Catholics in the community. This effort was bound to end in failure, and still further aggravate the situation. The Catholic Church may rightfully lay claim to a long and illustrious past, but in this instance one of its leaders was opposing something that is older by far than the Church itself, older perhaps than man himself, the sense of community. The Czechs were neighbors before they were Catholics, and neighbors they will be whether they belong to a church or not.

Since the priest left the community the dividing line which he created has all but disappeared. The new priest is a kindly person whose parents were born in Bohemia. He understands the temperament of his people. He knows that they can be led but not driven. His greatest contribution to the community life thus far has been the development of a young people's dramatic society. He has helped in the production of several plays given in the Czech language. He gives people the impression that he is one of the community, instead of one against it.

The Protestant Church in Milligan

When one turns from the activities of the Catholic Church to that of the one Protestant church which has been brave enough to try to convert the inhabitants of Milligan, he finds a very different picture. The Methodist Church has tried vainly to establish itself in the town. It has never been able to support a full-time minister, and has had to depend upon the services of ministers who are located in neighboring towns. Services have been held for the adult members of the community at various hours on Sunday morning, but regardless of when the services were held the attendance was so small as to discourage even the most optimistic of ministers. At the time this study was conducted there remained only a Sunday School for children held on Sunday morning. Attendance at this Sunday School had never been good, and for the past two years its numbers had been dwindling.

The type of work which is carried on in the Sunday School is illustrated by the following quotations:

"Children's services which will do good to older children, at 10 A. M. Sunday School at 11 A. M. Come and bring others. Special music for the services of two violins and piano.

"It will not do to complain about the youth.   Give them a good example and attend church services somewhere.   Don't make only living, but life.

"It is necessary for a good future to have a good beginning.   We have secured a Scoutmaster, and we would like to see how many boys are ready to join the Scouts in Milligan.   Come Sunday and enjoy a good crowd, worshipping the Lord of all."[12]

The Scoutmaster may have been ready, but the Scouts were not, and nothing ever came of this attempt to interest the young.   The next quotation describes some of the other attempts made to interest the children.

"The Sunday School work is going on very nicely considering the cold and disagreeable weather we have been having.

"Each Sunday the children are given a chalk talk or object sermon by the pastor.   If you have not been attending you should come and enjoy these with the Sunday School.

"Interesting hand work is being done by the small children and all the classes are doing good work.   It is a splendid place to go for three things: For the social fellowship, for the enjoyment of the morning hours, and for the knowledge of the Scriptures that is given."[13]

Adults and children are both appealed to in the following quotation:

"Men are known by the way they walk, talk, and balk.   The kind of ancestors we have had is not as important as the kind of ancestors our descendants have.

"Sunday, August 1, at 9:15 A. M., come to the Z. C. B. J. Hall and ride with us to Tobias, where Dr. J. B. Gettys will preach.   You will hear something worth your while and it may change you and your life.

"Catechism will be taught every week from now on.   Wednesday, July 28, at 3 P. M., we will meet in Mr. and Mrs. Michener's home. Every child needs religious training.   Send or bring your sons and daughters for we want to teach every child to honor the father and mother, as the Holy Book is teaching us.   Bible study at 2 P. M. in Mr. and Mrs. Smith's home.   Every welcome to come among us at any time."[14]

It is apparent from the names in the above quotation that the leaders among the Methodists of Milligan are non-Czechs. Indeed, many of them believe that there would be no Protestant religious service held in Milligan if it were not for their efforts.

One of the many ministers who have worked in the Milligan community stated his purpose as follows:

"In order that there may be no misunderstanding of our motives and aims in carrying on our work let us state that our motive is to try with all our might to live as Christ lived in principle and to teach

[12] *Nebraska Signal*, February 4, 1926, p. 5.
[13] *Nebraska Signal*, December 6, 1928, p. 5.
[14] *Nebraska Signal*, July 29, 1926, p. 5.

others to do so. Our method may seem peculiar and unlike other methods, but if so, please remember we are only trying to satisfy the hunger of our souls for all the knowledge and fellowship of Christ that we can gain. We believe Jesus is the only pure example of God's nature and that He came to lead us to be like God. It is our great desire to find complete satisfaction for our souls by following Christ's example. All who are of like mind are cordially invited to unite with us in our services every Sabbath morning in the Z. C. B. J. Hall. Preaching 9:30 to 10:30. Sunday School immediately following."[15]

In the above quotations evidences may be found that the Methodist Church in Milligan is on the defensive. In one of the quotations it is implied that men balk. It is certainly true that the men of Milligan balk at being led into a Protestant church. Christianity as a way of life is emphasized, but Christianity as a road to salvation is seldom mentioned in the church notices. The children's classes are encouraged to compete for new members by the offer of prizes to the class which brings in the largest number in any one month. Scouting and hand work are used to get children to come to worship. In spite of all methods used, the church remains empty. "They've driven out all the Protestant churches which were started in Milligan," said one of the non-Czech farmers. The failure of the Protestant churches in Milligan is easily understood. Most of the ministers have been non-Czechs. The strongest adherents of the Protestant church in Milligan are non-Czechs. There is little understanding on their part of the temperament of the Czech people. There is even a stubborn unwillingness on their part to attempt to understand it. They are a small religious group in a world of agnostics. The worldly success of the agnostics develops in some of the unsuccessful non-Czechs a feeling of inferiority. The belief that they have found the way and the life while so many about live in darkness is flattering to their ego. And so, while they bewail the fact that the church does not prosper in Milligan, secretly they are glad that it makes no progress. While at first glance it would appear that the non-Czechs are the backbone of the church without which it would not survive, actually they are indirectly responsible for its failure. If they were to withdraw and if someone who understood the temperament of the Czech people were to take charge he would find fertile ground on which to sow the seeds of his church. The Czech people are not atheistic or anti-religious, but many of them are opposed to the form in which religion is offered to them at present. Their bitter experience in Bohemia has taught them the necessity for the separation of Church and State, and they

15 *Nebraska Signal*, February 24, 1927, p. 5.

are eager to help solve the problem of the proper place of the church in the life of the community.

Church Membership of Non-Czechs in Milligan

While some of the non-Czechs work very zealously in the interests of the Methodist Church, not all of them do so. Of 53 non-Czechs, 19 reported that they did not belong to any church, 12 Catholic, eight were Methodist, six German Lutheran, one Congregational, and one Presbyterian, two Latter Day Saints, two United Brethren and two belonged to a Community Church.

Attitudes Toward Religion in Milligan

Many of the Czechs as well as the non-Czechs believe that Milligan needs a second church, but the reasons offered differ somewhat. The non-Czechs usually believed that a new church would make the community a better place in which to live. To their minds a church exerts a great moral influence in the community. If they were asked to be specific they would reply that a church would insure better observance of the Sabbath or that it would tend to decrease the amount of intoxicating liquor consumed by the community. "Most of the people in Milligan don't know what Sunday means," said one of those who thought another church would help Milligan to become a better place in which to live.

Most of the Czechs thought that Milligan was rather a good town as it was. A few, however, thought that a church would make it better. This opinion was held pretty generally by those who had been born and brought up in Milligan, and then had gone elsewhere to live. In these other communities they found the church a pleasing association. A few of the more thoughtful members of the community believed that a church should be installed in Milligan because most of the children were growing up to manhood without a knowledge of the Bible and the literature which has grown up about it. "One of our boys moved away from Milligan. One day he read aloud to his class in school a story from Job. He had never heard about the unfortunate old boy in the Bible, and he pronounced the word as though it had a small letter. He had heard of men getting jobs, but not of Job. All the other children in the room snickered at his mispronunciation. Now, if he had been able to learn Biblical stories here in Milligan he would not have made the mistake he did and would not have felt embarrassed. After all, Christianity and the Bible

are a part of our culture, and everyone ought to know something about them."

Although a large proportion of the inhabitants of Milligan
do not belong to any church, and a great many of those who
do belong do not attend church with any degree of regularity,
there is very little anti-religious feeling in the community.
Several years ago a large audience in Geneva, the county seat,
listened to a bitter and salacious attack on the Catholic Church.
The opinion of the Milligan community is well expressed by
the Milligan correspondent in the following article which
appeared in the next issue of the county newspaper:

"The Geneva city auditorium will house and seat more people than
any other building in the county. When we hold a democratic convention there the handful of the faithful gathered to worship at the
shrine of justice and equality in government rattle in the big structure
like a pea in a cream can. Not enough interest has ever been aroused
in governmental affairs to fill the spacious hall.

"On other occasions we have been in attendance there on Memorial
Day when we met for the purpose of honoring the dead. But no
memorial gathering has ever been so vast that the auditorium would
not accommodate the throng.

"Finally, however, there came a day when a topic of absorbing
interest did draw a crowd that not only filled the place from cellar to
garret but left many standing on the outside bewailing the loss of an
opportunity to listen to the sentiments which tickled the palate and
caused the heart to beat with a flutter of ecstasy and the mouth to
water at suggestions the realization of which comes only once in a lifetime. The speaker of the occasion was a woman. For her subject she
chose a religious sect organized for the purpose of glorifying God and
serving humanity. And the substance of her talk was of such a nature
that for an afternoon meeting only women were allowed to be present
and the evening was as salacious as the law would allow, the speaker
suggesting glibly that it was not necessary for her to repeat the lecture
of the afternoon because she knew that the women who had attended
had already repeated it for her. What a fine, delicate compliment for
the women present at the afternoon meeting.

"Whether or not the woman was telling the truth is beside the
question. If she was telling the truth, her business was to be telling
it before a court and a jury instead of before a horde of men and
women who would have blushed in shame to have repeated the story
in the presence of their sons and daughters. The scene was laid in
territory where the highest official was one who was prejudiced against
the sect which she attacked. Surely he would not have hesitated to
help redress whatever wrongs were being committed against God and
against society. But she preferred to tell her story to thirsting and
hungry audiences all over America at twenty-five cents a listen.

"One must come to the conclusion that human nature is much the
same as it was two thousand years ago. The glorious and the beautiful we approach with halting step but show us the mire and the slime
and we, grinning from ear to ear, reach for it struggling like mad to
make sure that not a single, tiny morsel shall escape us. On this
occasion, the woman had for her subject one particular religious sect.
When her mate comes along in time with a similar salacious story
of some other sect, the interest will be just as intense. We read with

horror of the crucifixion of Christ and wonder what manner of men and women must have lived in the age when this deed was done, but the truth is that they were not much different from those of today. Were the scene to be re-enacted, there would be found those ready to fill the roles of the persecutors and among those who attended the meeting at Geneva might be some who in the lead of the crowd would bellow with voices hoarse and terrible, 'Crucify Him, Crucify Him.' "[16]

Religion occupies a different place in Milligan than it did in a typical Czech village in the old world. Public opinion in the town is on the side of non-conformity rather than con-formity. There is no pressure exerted by the government. Each may go his way as he chooses. The bitter opposition which arises where pressure is applied is lacking. Neighbors of different faiths or of no faith may dwell together in peace.

Criticism has often been raised against Czech immigrants in America on the ground that they are non-religious. How-ever, their opposition to the church has been based more largely on political than on religious grounds. They have contended that the church should render unto Caesar the things that are Caesar's, and concern itself only with God. They have held tenaciously to the belief that men should be free to think as they pleased. Real thought is impossible without knowledge, and all the avenues of knowledge must be open to one who seeks the truth.

The tenacity with which the Czech holds to what he con-siders the truth is illustrated by an incident which occurred during the summer of 1930. One dull Sunday evening the streets of the village were the scene of a controversy between two older men over an issue of the day. The argument pro-ceeded from words to blows. After the battle was over the victor retired to his room while the vanquished sat on the doorstep holding his bleeding head in his hands. While his landlady busily washed up the blood on the sidewalk she upbraided him severely for fighting in public. "It's a shame, that's what it is, it's a shame," she said. From the doorstep the man replied with conviction, "I'll stand up for the truth even if he kills me." This fanatical desire to hold to what he considers to be the truth has characterized the attitude of the Czech toward religion. In America he is free to pursue the truth as he sees it. When he came to the new world his pur-suit of the truth carried him far to the left in matters of reli-gion. The pursuit has not ended in the new world, and the future may witness a movement back to the church. On only one point will the Czech remain firm. Church and State must not be one. Force may be used by the State to achieve its

[16] *Nebraska Signal*, April 2, 1925, p. 5. Written by a Czech non-Church member.

legitimate ends, but the Church must remain a free and voluntary association which man joins because it serves to satisfy his desires and fulfill his needs. This vision was held by the founders of America; in its realization the Czech is determined to aid.[17]

---

[17] It is highly probable that religious conditions similar to those prevailing in Milligan are to be found in many Czech communities in America, though not in all of them. In some communities, such as Brainard, Nebraska, an able and enterprising priest has succeeded in building a strong and powerful Catholic Church. However, Czech communities such as these are the exception rather than the rule. Conditions such as prevail in Milligan are not typical of non-Czech communities in this section of Nebraska. Ohiowa, a neighboring village with about the same population as Milligan, has three very active churches, two Lutheran and one Methodist. A large proportion of the population of Ohiowa is of German descent. Both of the Lutheran pastors were born in Germany. It is reasonable to conclude that religious conditions in Milligan are due to the fact that it is a Czech community, and that similar conditions will usually be found wherever Czech immigrants have settled. Cf. Edmund de S. Brunner, *op. cit.*, Chapter V.

CHAPTER VI

BOOK-LEARNING OLD AND NEW

"The time is fast approaching when the school bell will ring again and the children will be wending their way to the training quarters like a line of soldiers. . . . Now is the time when the boy and girl from the country, having completed the eighth grade in their district, are looking about for a school to enter in the fall. To all such we extend an invitation to plan to come to the Milligan school. Our school is fully accredited. Besides the regular academic courses, we offer the normal training course, the agricultural course and domestic science with manual training. The latter is under the supervision of the Federal government, being known as the Smith-Hughes work. The boys have a regularly organized high school band and altogether we believe that our schools offer better advantages and facilities than any other school in the community. We invite the young people from the country to examine carefully into the many advantages and conveniences that our schools offer and assure them that we shall be glad to have them in our student body."[1]

Milligan School Activities

The principal and two of the four elementary teachers of the school are of Czech extraction. In 1924 the annual school meeting instructed the board to arrange for the teaching of Bohemian in the high school "if it could be done without interfering with the required high school course of study." The Czech language has been taught rather irregularly since. It is offered only if one of the teachers is competent to teach it, if there is a demand for it, and if it does not interfere with the course of study.

The five high school instructors, all non-Czechs, teach a curriculum consisting of Latin, English, mathematics, science, history, agriculture, and vocational and normal training. All of the high school and one of the elementary teachers are college graduates. None of them have done any post-graduate work. Two of the elementary teachers have attended college for two years and the other for three.

Lessons and social affairs both claim the time of the students. During the year 1929-30 one pageant, three plays, and one cantata were offered by students in the school and were well attended by the parents. One of the yearly entertainments is described in the following article:

"On the evening of December 22nd at the high school auditorium, the grade pupils rendered one of the nicest Christmas programs that has ever been given here. They presented a cantata, 'The Santa Claus Trail,' and everyone of those little ones carried out their parts beyond

[1] *Milligan Times*, July 27, 1920, p. 1.

one's expectation, and the costumes and scenery were superb. The
Milligan high school orchestra furnished the numbers between the acts.

"The closing number was the pantomime, 'Silent Night,' which was
very impressive. This followed the usual distribution of the Christmas
treat' to each pupil. The auditorium was filled to capacity, much of the
standing room being taken."[2]

There is the usual round of class parties and banquets.
The school has a number of clubs, centering for the most part
about music and farming. The agricultural club is one which
arouses great interest on the part of the members.

"The Milligan Ag. Club held its third monthly meeting at
the home of Mr. Kovanda on Tuesday evening with President Uldrich
in charge. . . . This month's question for discussion was, 'Is it
better to plant or list corn?' The business session was followed by
amusements and luncheon. The county agent will give a talk and show
a movie to the Ag. Club at its January meeting.

"During the month of December our department has culled seven
hundred chickens, vaccinated eighty hogs, spliced two hay ropes,
diagnosed and prescribed treatment for two cases of poultry disease,
and supplied bulletins to three local farmers. We are anxious to increase the service of our department to the community.

"The rural economics class drove to Geneva Wednesday to hear
Mr. Brokaw talk on the corn borer. They also saw our state champion
bread-baking team give a demonstration. Stick to it, Irene and Helen,
the Ag. boys are mighty proud of you!"[3]

Through the students in its department of vocational agriculture the Milligan school attempts to help the farmers of
the community, but a more direct method of aiding the
farmers is also employed. A special evening course is offered,
in which is taken up various problems confronting the
farmer.

"An invitation has been extended to the farmers of the neighborhood to enroll for ten lectures on any agricultural subject they may
choose. As many as three classes may be organized. One of these
will probably be a class of women taking up the subject of poultry
or similar work. No expense is attached on the part of those attending. The courses have been carried on at Friend and Daykin with
marked success, and it is hoped that Milligan will show an interest in
keeping with the spirit of the community."[4]

These classes are very popular. In 1925 courses were
offered in wheat, poultry, and beef production. They were
conducted in the form of open discussions. The members of
each class were invited to give their contributions to the
solution of the problems raised.

Occasionally outside speakers are brought in to address
the students in the school. During Education Week the stu-

[2] *Nebraska Signal*, December 29, 1921, p. 3.
[3] *Nebraska Signal*, December 29, 1927, p. 5.
[4] *Nebraska Signal*, January 8, 1925, p. 5.

dents are usually deluged with a stream of addresses. These are usually inspirational rather than informational.

"The school held a special convocation period program when speakers addressed the students on appropriate subjects. The first day Dr. V. V. Smrha talked to the students on the importance of good health.

"S. R. Elson, state director of adult education, spoke on the second day. He told the students what an education means to grown-ups, and how many didn't have the opportunities that people in school today have. On Wednesday the superintendent and principal spoke on the topics, 'The Other Fellow,' and 'Our Present Obligation.' Thursday's program was filled by Attorney Grady Corbitt, of Geneva. He gave an interesting talk along the lines of opportunities people have in school. He gave some good illustrations of men who had made use of these opportunities and how it affected them and those they came in contact with later.

"Friday was Armistice Day, so nothing could have been better than having Attorney Robert Waring speak to the students about the meaning of Armistice Day. He said Armistice Day was the day that marked the triumph of republican government over monarchial government. He explained that the old idea of people where the belief existed that some were born to rule was now defeated by the belief that all men were created equal. All men should have a voice in their government. He showed how school was the place to work hard and fit oneself for the place in this work of governing himself and helping govern the nation."[5]

If the students in the Milligan school fail to become successful men and women and good citizens, it will not be because they have had no advice. In addition to the inspirational talks of neighboring lawyers, a definite attempt is made to teach good citizenship in the classes. A system of rewards and punishments is used to create good citizens.

"Thursday each class held a meeting to elect a member to represent them in citizenship. . . . The four delegates met with the faculty to decide what the pupils with a citizenship grade of 95 or better should do during the recreational period. During the first recreational period, the last period Friday afternoon, outdoor games were played. Those pupils having a citizenship grade below 95 stayed in the assembly in charge of one of the teachers and learned how to be good citizens.

"Citizenship classes met Wednesday. The American creed and pledge to the flag were studied."[6]

Starting with 1919, all school children were examined for physical defects. The doctor made the following remarks: "Milligan is to be commended for having no parents who are neglecting their children's permanent teeth. Milligan children are suffering more from neglected eyes than from any other defect. In most cases neglected eyes were found to be accompanied by defective teeth, which in some cases have

⁵ *Nebraska Signal*, November 17, 1927, p. 5.
⁶ *Nebraska Signal*, November 14, 1929, p. 5.

been filled."[7]   Each year a health campaign is put on to interest parents with children who are about to enter school for the first time.   Pre-school children are examined and their defects called to the attention of the parents, who are urged to correct them as a preparation for school work.

The school possesses a gymnasium and some playground equipment for the smaller children.   About the only sport which succeeds at all well in the school is basketball.   There are not enough boys in attendance to develop an adequate football team.   Baseball has been played now and then by school teams.   As a rule, however, the school has not been very successful in so far as athletics are concerned.   Occasionally a good basketball team is produced, one which is able to win the county tournament.   When Milligan has one of its good teams, it usually raises money to send it to the state tournament.   The team is nearly always eliminated in the first round.   Even when they have a good team the boys receive poor support from the town.   "Our basketball boys turned in their tenth victory of the season when they trounced Cordova 28 to 6. . . . The game was played before an empty house.   It is unfortunate that our boys received such little support."[8]

At the close of the school year, commencement and class picnics attracted the attention of the students.   What would school be without a picnic!

After various class parties and banquets, the seniors find that their high school days are over.   Each year from ten to twenty-five boys and girls sit upon the platform and hear the words which sever their connection with the school and start them on their journey through life.

"The commencement exercises of the Milligan high school were held in the high school auditorium Thursday evening.   The stage was very prettily arranged for the occasion and the program went off without a hitch in a very creditable manner.   The class marched into the room and onto the stage in a very stately manner as Helen Bulin played a solemn march at the piano.   The room was filled with spectators and friends of the graduates, a number having to stand in the hall for lack of seats.   Even the amphitheatre in the rear of the room was filled to the ceiling.   Father Supik opened the ceremonies with invocation and closed with a benediction.   A class prophecy was given by Henrietta Bors.   The class will was read by Anton Hamouz.   Marie Buzek gave a history of the class.   Miss Bessie Selement sang a very pretty solo, and Marietta Walla gave an interesting reading, illustrative of the dances of long, long ago.

---

[7] *Nebraska Signal*, October 21, 1919, p. 8.

[8] *Nebraska Signal*, February 23, 1928, p. 5.   This condition is very different from that prevailing in Middletown, where the entire community is interested in the success of the high school basketball team.   Milligan will leave in a body to witness a Sokol tournament, but nearly all of the older members of the community see little to interest them in a basketball game.

"The speaker of the evening was Dean Heyhoe of Doane. His talk was a very interesting one. In it he emphasized the necessity of a sound body, a trained mind and the building of a good character as necessities for a successful life. The diplomas were presented by County Superintendent Margaret Haughawout in a few words in which she first congratulated the class on their achievement and then urged that they pursue their school work in some institution of higher learning. The members of the class were Helen Bors, Henrietta Bors, Marie Buzek, Anton Hamouz, Inez Kumpost, Joseph Kuska, Olga Kuska, James Tenopir, Mathias Novak, Mamie Simacek, and Rose Novak."[9]

And so another class, consisting almost entirely of Czechs, was turned out with the stamp of America on the brows of all its members. The pupils of the school are subjected to a standardized education, in the course of which their minds are molded to the common pattern of the new world. The school today is one of the agencies in the community most instrumental in changing its life. It supplies a ready-made set of answers to many questions confronting the young citizens. This was beautifully illustrated by one little girl, who, when asked if she believed in woman suffrage, replied, "I do not know. We haven't studied that in school yet."[10]

This marks a great change from the early Milligan. The slight effect which the little country school of fifty years ago had on its pupils at the time they were attending it all but vanished as they returned to the farms and the community in which they lived. Some of its former pupils cannot speak the English language today.

Milligan Schools in the Past

Ten immigrants who had been of school age both in Bohemia and America reported that settlement in the new world usually made it impossible for them to continue their education. Only one of them had attended high school, and he was one of the more recent arrivals who came after the country had been pretty well settled. Those who arrived when Milligan was young were put to work on the farm and attended the local school for not more than one year. One of these says today, "The old man put me to work as soon as we came to Nebraska. The teacher we had didn't know much and didn't care if we came or not. So we stayed at home and worked."

The first thought of the earlier immigrants to Nebraska was to secure land. They believed that the possession of a farm would enable them to realize their other desires—how-

[9] *Nebraska Signal*, May 26, 1921, p. 3.
[10] Cf. Chapter IV, p. 38.

ever, they soon discovered that the farm could be secured only at the expense of the education of their children. The land demanded work on the part of all members of the family, and the children were needed on the farm at an early age. The sacrifice involved is strikingly revealed in Table VI:

TABLE VI

EDUCATION OF INDIVIDUALS OF CZECH EXTRACTION, ALL OF WHOSE EDUCATION WAS SECURED IN THE UNITED STATES

	Group I First and second generation, ages 40 and over.	Group II Second and third generation, ages 21-39.	Group III Second and third generation, ages under 21.	
			Farm Children	Village Children
No education	3	0	0	0
Less than year	15	0	0	0
Attended but did not complete elem. school	60	15	2	0
Completed eighth grade only	22	43	8	0
Attended high school but did not complete twelfth grade	6	31	13	4
Completed twelfth grade only	6	38	10	9
Attended but did not complete college	2	19	1	0
Completed college	3	4	0	0
Completed normal school	1	0	0	0
Completed one year graduate work	0	1	0	0
Completed nurse's training	0	1	0	0
Still attending college	0	3	0	0
Still attending school	0	0	34	48
Total individuals	118	155	68	61
Median years at school	5.6	10.5	....	....

As will be seen from Table VI, the second group has had almost twice as much education as the first. Most of those in Group I secured their schooling before the village of Milligan was established. They had to work on the farm at an early age, and had little time for book-learning. Even today the farm tends to limit educational opportunities. The table shows that farm children receive less education than do village children.

Education in Bohemia of Immigrants to Milligan

Perhaps the greatest individual that Czechoslovakia has produced is Jan Amos Komensky—the famous Comenius. His contributions to the theory of education were made to the world, but his inspiration has guided the Czech people ever since his lifetime. Universal and compulsory education had been the law in Bohemia long before the first settlers in Nebraska left their homeland. The illiteracy rate among the Czech immigrants is very nearly the lowest among all groups which enter the United States.[11]

Eighty-two out of ninety first-generation inhabitants of Milligan educated in Bohemia had attended school until they were between ten and fourteen years of age.[12] Only two immigrants had spent less than two years in school; one of these was illiterate, while the other could read and write. Six had had education beyond the age of fourteen. One of these, who had come to America since the war, had been through high school and an architectural school. One had attended the elementary school until he was sixteen, one had attended high school for one year, and another for two years, while two had finished the "real gymnasium."

It was possible for the peasants of Bohemia to secure an elementary education, but it was very difficult to enter the institutions of higher learning. As one of the immigrants said, "I wanted to go to school and become a teacher, but my parents were poor. They could not send me to school after I was fourteen, and so they made me become a seamstress." The higher walks of life were open only to those who had attended the "gymnasium" and the university, and these educational facilities were closed to those who had no money. Those immigrants who stress education strongly, and who are ready to make every sacrifice to see that their children remain in school, do so not so much because they value education for itself, but because it is means to a better life. These means were not open to them in the old world, and so they came to the new in search of them.

College Education

The sentiment in favor of a college education for young folks is very strong in the community. Milligan sends many more students to the State University than does any other community in Fillmore County. "An actual count has revealed that of the Fillmore County students in attendance at the State University more than one-half came from Milligan."[13] About one-twelfth of the population of the county

---

[11] Cf. Annual Reports of the Commissioner General of Immigration. Among 17,662 Czechs admitted in the years 1911–1912 the rate of illiteracy was 1.1 per cent.

[12] Of the total sample of 140 first generation, 90 received all their education in Bohemia, 40 received all their education in America, and 10 attended school in both countries.

[13] *Nebraska Signal*, November 22, 1928, p. 11. It is possible of course, that students from other parts of the county attended other universities in greater number than did Milligan students. It is difficult to determine if this is so, but the probabilities are that few Fillmore County youths attend other colleges than the State University.

live in the Milligan district. This strong interest in education among the Czechs of Nebraska conforms to the traditions of old Bohemia.

"Should children go to college? Why, of course they should. It makes them better citizens, and they can get better jobs." In some such manner would the average citizen of Milligan express his convictions with regard to a college education. But while the above speaker expresses the general opinion of the inhabitants, there is a considerable minority which would disagree very violently.

Perhaps a greater insight will be obtained into the mind of Milligan on this point if the inhabitants are allowed to speak in their own words. The first group of replies are those of individuals who have had little education themselves.

"They get more education and know everything more. They do better in life. You can never take education away from a person."

"All who have gone from this neighborhood amount to nothing. Better to teach boys a trade, girls to work."

"Children don't need even high school. I got along without it all right. Especially the girls do not need it. They get married and then what good is it. It makes children lazy."

"Some are helped and some are harmed. Some become robbers and thieves. This happens most often."

"Education is good. Giving my children an education kept me in town. In my day youngsters had to work hard."

"If one goes to college he gets a good education. Men need more education than women, but women too need an education. If the husband dies, she can work."

"Most successful business men have had a common school education."

"Children ought to be educated. It helps in lots of ways in life. I don't know how exactly."

"Maybe they want to be something else. If they don't go to college they can't be."

From the uneducated group came the largest number of those who did not believe that education was a good thing. While there were a relatively large number of dissenters in this group, they constituted a rather small minority in the group as a whole.

Those who had had little education belonged for the most part to the older age groups. The younger individuals in the community had had more education, and were much more certain that an education is very valuable.

"After graduation there will be more educated people and the country will prosper."

"It gives them better chances than others. It broadens their intellect. They meet different people. They meet problems better. They see a question from more sides than from one narrow viewpoint."

"Four years of early life mean nothing financially. They cannot save at this stage. During this period they are laying the foundations of their life."

"They have better opportunities to get what they are interested in. In high school they have little choice."

"Education does not hurt them. They get along a lot easier in the world, physically, mentally, morally. They are healthier and cleaner. They get an easier job, with better pay and shorter hours."

"Education is the best thing parents can give them. They get out of high school so young they don't hardly know what to do. They will have an easier time in life. They find it easier to solve problems."

Non-Czechs in Milligan were unanimous in their belief that children should go to college. The reasons which they gave for their opinions were much the same as those given by the Czechs.

Replies of individuals give flashes of insight into the mind of Milligan, but the public as contrasted with personal opinion can be gained only by considering the replies as a whole. Some 470 Czechs and 49 non-Czechs expressed themselves on this question. Of the 470 Czechs, 427 gave an unqualified yes as their answer, seven said that those children should go who would profit by a college education, three replied that they did not know, and 33 answered in the negative. Thirty-one of the 33 who answered in the negative were first- or second-generation individuals in the age group forty and over. First-generation men and women who answered in the negative constituted one-seventh of the total number in their age group; in the same age group in the second generation those who replied in the negative constituted one-fifth of the total number. Those who did not approve of college had not had much education themselves. Looking back over their own lives, these older people could not see how book-learning could have helped them. They had been unable to provide their children with a good education, but in most cases they had been able to give them farms. Of what need then to go to college? When these older people were asked what they would like to have that they did not now have, they very often replied, "I'd like to be living on my farm again." They were too old to be able to do so, but the fascination of the life they had lived there was still upon them. A lifetime of toil had made them love the work of the farm and they could not understand why the younger people wished to free themselves of the bonds of hard work which they loved. Education taught children to spend money rather than to save, and this also ran counter to the philosophy which had moved the older people throughout their lives.

Again, the older people who were opposed to an education knew little of any other way of life than their own. Their lack of understanding of the English language and the necessity of constant labor on the farm had made it impossible for them to leave the community in which they lived. Few people took any vacations in the Milligan of even thirty years ago If a vacation was taken, it consisted of a visit to relatives. These relatives lived either in a Czech agricultural community like Milligan, or in one of the Czech colonies in the city. While visiting these relatives they lived in the same narrow Czech culture in which they lived at home. If the general life of America touched them at all, it touched them in an undesirable way. The people whom they met on the trains and in the towns did not understand them; the newspapers which were sold in the city were printed in a language they could not read. They were glad to return to a community which contained neighbors who understood them, to an environment over which they had some control, to work which they loved.

"I don't want my children to have to work as hard as I do," was the motive which determined many Milligan parents to send their children to college. The children are one with their parents on this point. They don't want to face a life of hard work. Education is to them a means of escape. Of 262 individuals of all generations under forty, only two believed that children should not go to college.

From the individual replies given previously it is apparent that one of the chief reasons for going to college is that the student may secure a better living thereby. Perhaps they misjudge what education can do for them. Perhaps education will create more problems than it will solve, will bring new influences to play upon their lives, and cause the simple life of their ancestors to disappear in the rushing complexity which is the modern world. Nevertheless, they are determined to be on their way.

Many of the young people of Milligan have secured university degrees and gone elsewhere to work, as there is little opportunity in the community for the college-trained worker.[14]   Only seven individuals who have completed college have returned to Milligan to live.   There are also in the village twenty-one individuals who attended college but did not finish.   It may be inferred that those who did not succeed at academic work are the more likely to return.   This condition again is probably typical of American agricultural communities.

Knowledge of Czech and other Languages

Education is not confined to the curriculum of the public school, and a phase which is not revealed by the statistics thus far given concerns efforts to perpetuate the Czech language.   At various periods off and on attempts have been made to establish a "Bohemian school" in the village.   Classes were held once weekly in the local lodge hall.   It has been several years since the last of these schools died a death due to poor attendance.   Czech is now offered in the high school as an optional foreign language.   Enrollment in these classes has been sufficient to retain the subject in the school, but not enough to develop a real interest in Czech literature among the students.

In order to find out how the Czech language was surviving in Milligan, members of the second and third generations were asked to state how well they spoke, read, and wrote Czech.   The answers were then classified under the heads, "Well," "Little," "None."   A summary of these answers revealed that these inhabitants of Milligan are fairly proficient in speaking Czech, less proficient in reading the language, and least proficient in writing, and that the loss of the language has been greater among the members of the third generation than among the members of the second.

Ninety-eight per cent of the second generation speak the language fairly well or better, 37 per cent can read, and 25 per cent write it more or less well.   Whereas among the third generation 80 per cent can speak Czech fairly well or better, 12 per cent can read it, and seven per cent write it.

A change of this sort is to be expected in an immigrant community.   The spoken language survives longer because it is useful in the community.   Many of the inhabitants of Milligan speak English only with difficulty, and some of them do not speak it at all.   On the other hand, there is little real need for the written language.

A survey of the households shows that the Czech language is still the predominant means of family intercourse, but that

14 Cf. Chapter III,   pp. 18, 19.

in a number of the homes English has supplanted Czech, while in others both languages are used. In the latter households the parents usually speak Czech to each other, whereas the children speak English among themselves and to their parents. The results are summarized in Tables VII and VIII:

TABLE VII

LANGUAGES SPOKEN BY PARENTS IN HOMES IN MILLIGAN COMMUNITY

	Czech	English	Both	Total
First-generation homes	90	8	3	101
Second-generation homes	47	47	16	76
Total first- and second-generation homes	137	21	19	177
Village homes	86	14	11	111
Farm homes	51	7	8	66
Total village and farm homes	137	21	19	177

TABLE VIII

LANGUAGES SPOKEN BY CHILDREN IN HOMES IN MILLIGAN COMMUNITY

	Czech	English	Both	Total
First-generation homes	35	20	4	59
Second-generation homes	17	9	28	54
Total first- and second-generation homes	52	29	32	113
Village homes	21	19	22	62
Farm homes	31	10	10	51
Total village and farm homes	52	29	32	113

It is seen from the tables that the Czech language is slowly dying out in Milligan. The process has gone further in second-generation homes than it has in the first, and further in the village than in the country. In five households which represented mixed marriages, the English language was used exclusively.

Twenty-two older men and women, born in Nebraska during the pioneer period, speak the English language imperfectly, while one confessed that he knew no English whatsoever. These constituted about one-fourth of the second-generation individuals who were forty years and over.

Thirty-six persons in Milligan reported familiarity with foreign languages other than Czech; 22 of these belong to the first-generation group, 14 to the second. The latter had studied German, Latin, or Spanish in school. Twelve of them stated their knowledge of the language they had studied was very limited. One had a fair knowledge of German, gained to some extent by association with German people in this country, and one, the village priest, had a good knowledge of Latin. On the other hand, 11 of the first-generation group had a fair or good command of German, while 8 had understood it well in their youth, but had forgotten much of it in the years that had passed. Three had acquired a slight knowledge of other foreign languages—one knew a little Russian, one a little Croatian, and the other could speak some French. These 22 constituted about 15 per cent of first-generation individuals forty years and over. Other foreign languages thus seem to have even a harder time in Milligan than does Czech. Those which are taught in the schools make slight impression on the students. In time to come English will have triumphed over all its rivals, and the cultural elements which are associated with other languages will be lost in Milligan.

Analysis of Changes

The history of book-learning in the community is one of early vicissitude and later triumph. The generations passed through a cycle—the pioneers arriving in the new world with a thorough European education and a great tradition—the children going unschooled in a rough country—sacrificing cultural values to the demands of the land—and the children's children coming again in time into the spiritual heritage of their Bohemian forefathers. The new learning is American, however, in method and content, and is a force transforming old ways into new. In the education of the community, therefore, persistence and change are both present—since the spirit is of the old world—the substance of the new.

Summary

One of the most important influences producing change today is the Milligan public school. This is quite different from the early days when the country school was attended for only a few years or so by the children of the immigrants. Many of these children—now old men and women—can speak English but imperfectly and live unchanged in the narrow ways of their fathers. The adult immigrants came from Bohemia where a strong tradition of education existed and where a universal compulsory education law was in force. They had nearly all completed the elementary school and several had gone on to higher schools. It was difficult and unusual for the peasant in Bohemia to send his children to college, and opportunity for higher education was one of the causes for emigration. Hence, the sentiment for giving children a university education is very strong in Milligan. One of the chief reasons the people have for sending their children to college is to equip them for employment other than the hard labor they themselves have had all their lives. A minority group—the least educated—are strongly opposed to college education. These are mainly farmers and are distrustful of schooling. Milligan sends more young people proportionately to the State University than the rest of the county. Most of the graduates go elsewhere to work, but seven have returned to Milligan. Czech is still mainly spoken in the homes, but the younger people are using English more and more. There is little knowledge of other foreign tongues.

CHAPTER VII

IN THE HOME

"We Czechs are a great bunch of eaters. Take our favorite dinner, roast pork, sauerkraut, and potato dumplings. Any one of these dishes would give the average American indigestion for a week; put them all together before a Czech and he is in paradise."

Before the speaker was spread the dinner he described, and about the table were grouped the members of his family, all busily engaged in putting away huge quantities of their favorite dishes. At one end of the table stood a large dish heaped high with fresh "koláce," ready to be consumed with the inevitable coffee at the end of the meal. The preparation of food is still the central activity of the home, and the great time-consumer for the women. The Czech dishes require a high degree of skill and many hours of work, but the Milligan housewife has yet to relinquish any of her culinary duties to the restaurant or the baker.

Home Life

In all of the homes of Milligan the dining table draws the family together three times daily and helps determine the rhythm of its activities. The members who come together are clad in typical American clothes, factory-made or sewed at home to a popular pattern, but the table at which they sit is laden with dishes such as were eaten by their forefathers before the Battle of White Mountain. Less than one out of ten of the Czech households of Milligan are entirely on the American plan in respect to cooking and food. Eight out of ten specialize almost completely in Czech food, while in slightly more than one out of ten households the kitchen is on a fifty-fifty basis.

It is rather remarkable that the food habits should persist as strongly as they do. Czech dishes take a great deal of time and trouble to prepare, and many of them are highly indigestible. However, the Czech loves his food and his beer, and perhaps through the process of selection the Czech people have come to have good digestions.

While the food the people of Milligan eat is that of old Bohemia, the furnishings of the rooms in which they live are as modern as the house itself. In eight out of every ten Czech households of Milligan there are no material evidences of the old world. In a few of the homes photographs of the forest-clad mountains of western Bohemia or pictures of the frowning battlements of the Hradcany look down upon the latest products of Grand Rapids. Hidden away in the dresser drawers in some of the homes are pictures of relatives dressed in peasant costumes or beautiful examples of the delicate needlework which is the pride of the peasant housewife. A few bedrooms are decorated with pictures of the Virgin Mary or of Christ on the Cross. These pictures had been handed down from father to son or mother to daughter for many generations.

In these homes so strangely reminiscent of Bohemia in the food and so completely disconnected in material environment, Sunday is a great family institution. Sunday usually begins in Milligan with the members sleeping to a later hour than usual. This is especially true of the men-folk. After breakfast the women do the housework, while the men perform chores or work around the yard. When the Sunday papers come in work and worry are forgotten while the members of the family bury their noses in the sections of the newspaper which interest them. Few, indeed, go to church. After dinner is the time when the visiting begins. A visit does not mean a formal call lasting a few moments. It usually begins early in the afternoon and ends late in the evening. So many people go visiting in the afternoon that one wonders how they ever find anyone at home. Perhaps the secret lies in getting an early start!

Most of the visiting that is done is between families who are related to one another. Retired farmers spend Sunday with their children on the farm. Country people come into the village to spend the day with their town kinfolks. The whole family sets out together on these Sunday visits and are entertained by the entire family of the hosts. The men and women sit together—invariably indoors if in the village— and pursue endless conversations. Important world events receive scant attention and the talk turns tirelessly about the affairs of their friends and neighbors. Meanwhile, the children are engaging in play of their own invention in the house or yard.

Reading, resting, listening to the radio, fishing, fancy work, attending lodge meetings, movies, or dances, sports of various sorts, or loafing uptown are other diversions on a sleepy Sunday afternoon and evening. The long stream of automobiles which leave every American city on Sunday morning are missing in Milligan. Very few people in the town ever set out in their automobiles just for a ride. Perhaps it is the bad roads, or the poor scenery, or perhaps it is that the members of the community do not look upon the automobile as a means of enjoyment in and of itself.

Loafing uptown is a very popular pastime on a Sunday afternoon. All the stores except the drug store and the soft-drink parlors are closed, but the benches still line Main Street, and the old crowd of regular loafers is there. In the winter they fill the soft-drink parlors, and sit around talking or playing cards. A baseball game in summer will draw them away temporarily, but after the game is over they return to their places to discuss the play of the town team.

During the course of the week the people of Milligan have much less leisure time, but they spend it in somewhat the same way as they do their Sundays. There is perhaps less visiting. It takes a large piece out of the leisure time to get a family ready to go visiting. Visiting during the week is between individuals, rather than between families. The young people live not in one home but in all the homes of the community.

On winter evenings a popular pastime of the women folk is the stripping bee. From all over the community men and women gather at the home of some neighbor to assist her in stripping the feathers which she has been accumulating over a period of many months. Not even the bachelor homes in the community are immune from this sort of invasion. While the women strip the feathers in the kitchen, the men sit in the living room and play cards. Occasionally, instead of helping to make feather beds, the neighbors gather to make a quilt.

"About ten ladies met at the home of Mrs. A. A. Hamouz Thursday afternoon and again in the evening for the purpose of quilting a quilt in applique pattern of the wild-rose design. Both the afternoon and evening were spent profitably as well as enjoyably. Mrs. Hamouz served refreshments of kolace, cookies, wienies, pickles, and coffee. The quilting was so thoroughly enjoyed that more of it is planned during the winter."[1]

It was thought by the investigator before he went out to Milligan that some insight might be gained into the leisure-time habits of the various groups in Milligan if the people were asked where they saw their best friends. It was found soon after the investigation began that this question was useless, as far as finding out any differences in the way people spent their leisure time. For the community is really just one large family. The people know the homes of their neighbors as well as they do their own. The door is always open

1 *Nebraska Signal*, October 6, 1921, p. 3.

to the visitor, and it is opened often by him. There is a much greater feeling of neighborliness present in Milligan than there is in the average open-country community in America.[2]

The social isolation which the Bohemian pioneer found in Nebraska was a sore trial to him and the most frequent cause of complaint in those early days. An old lady who came from Bohemia as a little girl said of that period, "Here we just sat on Sundays." In the years which have passed the land has been subdued and the community has been created. In creating the community the pioneers followed the only model that they knew, the village community of Bohemia.

Most of the leisure-time activities of Milligan are still carried on in the homes. The all-embracing arms of the community are ever about the people; its ever-curious eyes are always upon them. The home and the community play the same important role in Milligan as they did in the little country villages of Bohemia.

In the old world the family in which the peasant lived was still pretty largely the patriarchal family in which his ancestors had lived for ages. The family was an economic as well as a social unit, and the father was the real head of the household. The fairs and festivals in which the family took part were closely associated with the work in which they engaged.

In Milligan the family has changed, but it has not changed as much as it would have if the immigrants had settled in the city. On the farm the family is still an economic unit, and even in the village the store is a family rather than an individual enterprise. All of the members work at the store as soon as they are old enough to do so. In leisure time, as we have seen, the family retains the chief importance.

It is beyond the scope of this study to discuss the subject of the family in its entirety, and an attempt is made only to consider the family as related to the changing social life of Milligan. The only external evidences of change in the family in the village are found in its decreasing size, in mixed marriages, and in those homes which have broken away from the established customs of the community.

Size of the Family

One of the reasons for migration from Bohemia was the fact that great poverty existed among the peasants. Associated with this poverty was usually found a large famliy of children. In order to determine the size of the average im-

---

[2] For an analysis of village and open-country communities see W. A. Terpenning, *Village and Open-Country Neighborhoods* (New York, 1931).

migrant family, first- and second-generation individuals twenty-one years of age and over were asked to state the number of children there were in the family in which they were reared. Data concerning 200 families were secured.[3] Of this number, 122 were families of individuals born in Europe, and 88 those of men and women who had been born in this country to parents born in Europe. In the first group the median number of children per family was 7.6; in the second group, 8.6. The difference between the medians is too small to be of any significance, in view of the small number of cases, but it is significant that in both groups families were large. There are too few third-generation individuals in Milligan whose parents had completed families to secure data that would be significant. However, it is highly probable that the families of this group will be much smaller in size than were the families of the other two groups. The village doctor reports that the annual number of births has declined about 50 per cent in the last thirty years. Children today do not have the economic value that they had in pioneer times. Farms were large and land was plentiful at that time. Standards of living were lower, and children did not demand an education. Today land has been divided among children to the point that further division would impair the efficiency of the farm. Village families have always been smaller than farm families, and today a large family is even a greater handicap than it was thirty years ago, when business in the village was expanding more rapidly than it is now. There is every reason, therefore, for the people to desire smaller families.

In order to determine the opinion of the community with respect to the optimum size of the family, each individual was asked to state the number of children the average family ought to have. Eight individuals refused to answer this question, or answered it with such expressions as "That rests with God." Catholics were especially averse to expressing an opinion on this subject. Some believed that the rich should have more children than the poor, although in Milligan itself the largest family, in which there are 13 children, is also the poorest.

Four hundred and sixty Czechs expressed a definite opinion on this point. Ten believed that the family should have no children, while one would set the limit as high as 10 per family. The other replies fell between these two extremes. The replies are summarized in Table IX.

---

[3] Care was taken not to duplicate data as to size of families in cases of brothers and sisters.

TABLE IX

OPTIMUM SIZE OF FAMILY

(As derived from opinions of 460 individuals)

No. of Children	Individuals belonging to				Individuals living		
	1st Gen.	2nd Gen.	3rd Gen.	Total	In village	On farm	Total
None	3	4	3	10	6	4	10
One	7	8	4	19	11	8	19
Two	18	66	21	105	53	52	105
Three	24	54	32	110	69	41	110
Four	45	76	19	140	82	58	140
Five	20	22	9	51	27	24	51
Six	5	9	1	15	7	8	15
Seven	1	1	1	3	1	2	3
Eight	3	2	0	5	4	1	5
Nine	0	1	0	1	0	1	1
Ten	1	0	0	1	1	0	1
Total	127	243	90	460	261	199	460
Median	4.2	3.8	3.5	3.9	3.9	3.8	3.9

It is apparent from this table that the people of Milligan believe that the average family today should have about one-half as many children as were to be found in the average family of a generation or two ago. The younger individuals would be content with a slightly smaller family than would be the older inhabitants. There is no significant difference between the opinions of those who live in the village and those who live in the country. If the Czechs of Milligan can have their way, the average family in the future will have three or four children, instead of seven or eight. This represents a change from conditions found in pioneer days and in the old world.

Mixed Marriages

Six of the households in Milligan consist of second-generation Czechs who have married non-Czechs. In five cases the husband is Czech, while in one case it is the wife who comes from Czech stock. All of the persons in these households were born in Nebraska. One of the families was that of a village bootlegger, and no data could be secured on this family. In four households the parents live together; in one case the wife of German extraction is divorced from her husband of Czech extraction. In four of the five families on which data could be secured the parents are all under the age of thirty. A total of 16 people lived in these homes.

Three of the five families rented the houses in which they lived, two of them owned their own homes without mortgages.

In all five families the English language was spoken exclusively. In none of the homes were there any Czech decorations or furnishings. In one of the households the wife had some garnet pins which had come from Bohemia. In two of the families the cooking consisted of Czech dishes, in two of American dishes, and in one Czech and American in about equal proportions. When it is realized that in only one of these households was the wife of Czech extraction it is apparent that the love of Czech food survives rather strongly, and often induces the non-Czech wife to learn a new and difficult method of cooking. In none of the households was any Czech newspaper, magazine, or book taken in the past year.

These families spent their time on Sundays much as did the others in Milligan. In the mornings the men worked about the house while the women did their house work. In the afternoon visiting, entertaining visitors, picnicking, reading, and sewing occupied their time. In the evening the movies proved to be a very great attraction. Seven of the nine adult members of these households went to the movies on Sunday evening. Radio, reading, and dances were other possible pastimes.

Only one of the members of these households attended any religious activities on Sunday. This member consisted of one boy aged seven years who went to the Methodist Sunday School. Both the father and the mother in this family were Catholic. The boy could not go to the Catholic Church because he spoke no Czech.

Except for the family in which a divorce had occurred, there were few tensions to be found. The non-Czech members fitted into the community life; the relationship between children and parents was normal. More of the old-world culture had been lost, but its loss had entailed no great conflict.

While the mixed marriages which exist in Milligan have been fairly successful, the Czechs in the community do not look with great approval on this practice. They especially disapprove if a Czech girl marries a non-Czech farmer. As one housewife expressed it:

"I do not believe in mixed marriages. Two of my sisters married American farmers and the marriages have not been very successful. Both of my sisters work very much harder than do other sisters who have married Czech farmers. They go out and work in the fields, and their husbands are only too glad to let them. You know, American women have an easy time of it because they are wise and know how to handle their husbands. They will not work any more than they have to, and they make their husbands afraid they will overwork. It is the wife who sees to it that she does little work, and when they go into marriage, our Bohemian girls who are used to hard work expect to work hard. They usually do, but the average Czech husband tries to conserve her strength and does not let her work in the fields. Not so with American husbands. They let their wives work in the fields, and for the most part the Bohemian wives of American husbands work much harder than those married to Czechs."

Unusual Homes

There are in Milligan only two individuals who have been divorced. One of these is a non-Czech who was married to a non-Czech. The husband lives in the village, while his former wife lives in another state. Their twenty-one-year-old daughter spends part of each year with one parent and part with the other. The other divorced person is a non-Czech whose former husband was a Czech. She lives in one of the large houses in the village, together with an unmarried daughter of about thirty years of age. On the whole the community expresses but little disapproval of divorced people.

A graver breach of the mores of the community occurred several years ago. A wife whose mental eccentricities had been a trial and tribulation to her long-suffering husband died and left him free to live as he pleased. For a time he enjoyed his freedom by visiting friends and relatives in various cities, but after a time this life palled on him, and he returned to his home in Milligan. A member of the opposite sex attracted him very much. Unfortunately for him, the good lady had a husband who was and still is confined in a nearby institution. Marriage was impossible as long as the husband lived. A solution of the problem was reached when the lady agreed to live with him as his housekeeper. For a time the community refused to accept this solution, but as the years passed it became adjusted to the situation. Today there is little social disapproval visited upon these two individuals. Perhaps the adjustment was made more easily because the two people concerned did not care very much what the community thought of their actions.

A somewhat similar case occurred when an elderly widow hired a young man half her age to act as her chauffeur and

handy man. The young man had been very well educated in
Bohemia, where his life had been spent in cities. He had
come to this country several years before, and traveled exten-
sively about the United States before coming to Milligan.
Nothing in America seemed to please him; no job that he
secured satisfied him. He longed to return to Bohemia, but
for some reason he was unable to do so. The widow liked him,
and the work he had to do required but little time or energy.
His situation did not please him much more than it did the
widow's neighbors, but he could think of no way of improv-
ing it. The neighbors were displeased for three reasons, and
it is difficult to determine which of these weighed most
heavily with them. In the first place, it was a most un-
orthodox relationship. In the second place, the disparity between the ages of the two individuals was very great. Finally, the young man was a most pronounced freethinker. Indifference to religion rather than active opposition to it char-
acterizes the attitude of most of the inhabitants of Milligan.
The young man made himself rather obnoxious by his in-
sistence on bringing religion into every conversation he had
with people in the village. The hostility of the neighbors was
abated somewhat late in the summer of 1930, when the widow
and the young man were united in marriage. Even this step
will not make is possible for the couple to fit into the social
life of the village very well. Fortunately for them, the widow
possesses a great deal of money, and much of their time is
spent traveling.

'There were a few other homes in Milligan which were not
quite normal, but only one of these came into conflict with
the mores of the community. This was the home of the most
important bootlegger. The respectable people of Milligan
were greatly displeased with his activity, and visited their
hostility on his entire family. He found it difficult to associate with his neighbors, and distrusted them all.

In another home lived an old lady who was mentally de-
ranged. She had driven her husband to another state, but
always imagined that he had just gone uptown for a few
hours. She lived a very isolated life. Several of the houses
in the village were occupied by bachelors or widowers. Most
of them were quite normal, but two of them lived rather
wretched lives. One of these was an old bachelor of sixty-
five, who found nothing in life to interest him, and wanted
to die as soon as possible. The other, a widower, was the
village shoemaker. He had come to the village a few years
before in response to an advertisement in a Czech newspaper.
He was laboring under delusions of persecution. He felt that

everyone in the village was opposed to him, and believed that the most innocent remarks were directed at forcing him to leave the village. A violin which he played rather badly was his great consolation and the only real criticism which his neighbors had to make against him.

Analysis of Changes

At one time the family was a community. All of the life of the individual was passed in it; all of his wants were taken care of by it; the beginning and the end of life were found in it. This patriarchal sort of family has now passed away in the city civilization of the modern world, and the family has become an association instead of a community.[4] It is only within the last thirty or forty years that other associations took over functions formerly performed by the family in Middletown.[5] This transition has gone much further in the city than it has in the country; it has gone much further in Middletown than in Milligan. There has been some differentiation of the social structure in Milligan, but this process has not gone very far and has affected the family but little. The school instead of the family educates the children today, and this change hastened the loss of the Czech language and has served to create interests in the children which cause them to leave the community. As far as religion is concerned, the church has lost out to the family rather than the family to the church. The organizations which in the city have taken away from the family its function as an agency in the use of leisure time hardly exist in Milligan. The lodge is perhaps the strongest leisure-time association in Milligan. It exerts a very strong influence over the lives of the people, but not much of the time of the people is spent in attending its meetings. Too, its influence has been exerted for the most part in the maintenance of the old-world traditions and folkways. Thus outside associations have not taken away from the family many of its functions. It is doubtful that the future will see any greater tendency on their part to do so. The form and functions of the family in Milligan will remain much as they are today. Within these limits the character of the family life may change. The English language will replace the Czech, English newspapers, magazines, and books will replace Czech publications, the members of the family will lose their eagerness to listen to Czech music over the radio, contract bridge may take the place of "darda," and in count-

---

[4] Cf. R. M. MacIver, *Society, Its Structure and Changes* (New York, 1931), Chapter VII.
[5] R. S. and H. M. Lynd, *Middletown* (New York, 1929), Chapter XIX.

less other ways the life lived within the family may change. Some of the children will drift away from the home, but not so much because of tensions existing in the relations between parents and children, as because of the irresistible attraction of the great city.   But the place of the family in the lives of those who remain in Milligan will not change very much. The singing of "Domov Muj" will awaken in the hearts of the people the old loyalties and the home will continue to be the one great agency which evokes their being and molds their lives.

CHAPTER VIII

YOUTH AND AGE

Mary Kovanda

Mary Kovanda is a widow of seventy-one. In 1873, when she was fourteen years old, her parents left Bohemia for the United States.

Mary attended school until she was eleven, when her father, a small farmer, needed her to work at home. She learned to speak the Czech language well, read it fairly, and write it a little. In this country she has learned no English. "I never went among American people, and there was no school I could attend."

In the half century or more since her parents left Bohemia, Mary has forgotten much of her life in the old world. "I don't even think of Bohemia. We had bad times there. Here in America we had a farm and property." However, although America has been good to her from an economic viewpoint, her success was gained at the cost of very great hardships. When asked what radio programs she enjoyed, she replied, "None. I have never enjoyed myself in America. I cannot enjoy it." She added, "If I were young and had to go through all I have been through, I would not want to be young but old today."

Ever since her husband died eight years ago Mrs. Kovanda has been living in a little house which her sons built for her in Milligan. She likes living in the village. "I am satisfied. It is a small town; there is no dust. There are some old men and women here. We do not notice others and they do not notice us." She could think of no changes which ought to be made in Milligan. "None; better heads would know." The young people, likewise, are pleasing to her. "No changes; everyone is good as he is." Nor does she have any desires which remain unfulfilled. "I do not want anything more."

Mrs. Kovanda has voted but once. "I will never vote again. My candidate did not win." She does not believe in women's suffrage. "Women have their own affairs. Men are wiser than women. Women should stay out. Men only should hold office."

Her two sons completed high school, but did not want to go to college. "I wanted my sons to go to college, but they did not want to go. They had farms, and liked to raise a family.   Children should go to college if they are capable, but they should not be forced."

In the declining years of her life, Mary Kovanda has found peace and contentment.   Her neighbors are old people like herself, and they live in a little world of their own.   They come into contact with the general life of the community but seldom.   Once or twice a year they attend a bazaar or a Bohemian play.   Dances they never attend.   "What an idea, an old grandmother!"   Mrs. Kovanda attends the Catholic Church occasionally on Sundays.   Neither of her sons are church members, but this fact does not worry her in the least.

Nearly all of the day she visits or dreams about the past. A Czech newspaper is the only publication which she receives. She borrows some reading matter from her neighbors, but in the past year she read no book.   The long years which she spent on the farm have made her rather shy and afraid of meeting people.   She is content to remain on the little street which forms a back-eddy in the life of Milligan.   Here, surrounded by the comforts of the present, she dreams of the hardships of the past and communes with those who helped to share them with her.

Old Man Hromadka

Old man Hromadka was born in Bohemia in the year 1854. His father was a blacksmith.   When the lad was old enough he learned his father's trade.   Soon after he became afflicted with the wanderlust.   "I wandered all over Europe.   I wanted to see how America was.   I heard times were good here, although one had to work.   I could work hard.   When I landed I came to Nebraska with three friends who were going west. I was twenty-two when I came to Nebraska.   I set up a blacksmith shop, and made good money."

Since coming to America Mr. Hromadka's world has revolved around money.   In his blacksmith shop he beat iron and steel into dollars.   From his shop and his farm he was able to make enough money to give each of his seven children $10,000 upon marriage.   He misses nothing in America.   "I have everything I need."   Of all that he found in America he likes best "everything that makes money."   He writes very little to the old world.   "I don't write so much now.   My relatives want money all the time."

While money has been the great love of his life, he has had other interests.   In following his trade he did not sacrifice his farm.   The love of the soil, which is in every peasant, has been with Mr. Hromadka throughout his life.   Since he retired to live in the village he has continued his agricultural labors. Every foot of the large lot he owns is under cultivation. He grows nearly all the vegetables he consumes. He spends a great deal of time on his fruit trees.

He is fairly well satisfied with Milligan. "I am well off; I don't worry about others. There are good people and bad here as elsewhere." The only improvement he thought could be made was the return of the saloon to Main Street. "We need saloons again. There would be no drunkards then. The town would get license fees, and have money. Now it owes money." The young people are all right, except that they spend too much money. "They chase girls in autos; they are always on the go. It will be bad here in time. Everyone wants a car." In his daughter's family there are six children and five cars.

The old man has little time for visiting. Occasionally his children or grandchildren come to see him. He almost never leaves his own home. From the time he awakens early in the morning until he goes to bed early in the evening he is busy. When the investigator called he heard a great deal of pounding going on in the rear part of the house. On the back porch he found Mr. Hromadka engaged in mending his shoes. Mr. Hromadka seldom wears shoes in summer, but he likes to have them in good repair in case of need. All day long he works barefoot in his garden or his orchard. Loafing on the benches uptown would be the last thing he would choose to do. When death finally comes it will no doubt find old man Hromadka with a hoe or pruning hook in his hands.

Katherine Smrha

Katherine Smrha is a widow, aged eighty-three. Some fifty years ago she came to America with her husband and her children. The new world has dealt very kindly with her family. Her children are all successful, and the declining years of her life are quiet and peaceful.

Most of the day Mrs. Smrha spends working about her house and her garden. She is a devout Catholic, and attends the village church regularly. Whenever fairs or bazaars are to be given Grandma Smrha gives cheerful assistance. None of her children or grandchildren belong to the Catholic Church. However, Grandma Smrha is very tolerant, and loves her children too much to find fault with them. When her husband died she insisted that his funeral services be conducted by the lodge rather than by the church, for fear that the political career of one of her sons would be injured.

Grandma Smrha spends a great deal of time reading and doing fancy work. She is very proud of her crocheting and knitting. Her body is bent from work, but her serene and kindly face shows that the troubles which have been her lot have not greatly disturbed her inner life. She possesses tolerance, sympathy, understanding. She loves her village and its people, young and old.

Mr. and Mrs. Janousek

Across the street from Mrs. Kovanda live Mr. and Mrs. Janousek. Mr. Janousek is eighty-three years of age, while his wife is two years his junior. The first time the investigator called on Mr. and Mrs. Janousek he was unable to make known to them the purpose of his visit. He called again after he had made several visits in the neighborhood. By this time the old couple had been informed of the nature of the investigation and were ready to give their answers. That is, Mrs. Janousek was; her husband was in a back room sleeping. Mrs. Janousek took the visit very seriously, and tried to tell the whole truth. Then she went into the back room to awaken her husband. He protested feebly at being awakened. "Don't grumble. You must come out and answer the gentleman's questions." And come Mr. Janousek did, rubbing his eyes and stretching his limbs.

In 1873, the couple were married in the little village in which they lived in Bohemia. Nine years later they left for America, acting upon the advice of relatives who lived there. Neither of them can speak a word of English. Mr. Janousek knew German in his youth, but he has forgotten it now.

They have never regretted leaving Bohemia. "There was poverty there. Here we had our own farm, and made a good living. I like it here better than in Bohemia."

They have no radio. If they had one, they would listen only to Czech music. They spend their days reading, visiting, or sleeping. If they had an extra hour a day, they would lie down and sleep it away. They enjoy living in Milligan because the children are near. Mrs. Janousek could suggest no changes which ought to be made in Milligan, but Mr. Janousek would like to see the saloon return. "I could do without prohibition." Both of them believe that the young people are too extravagant. "They do not work enough. They spend money; do not save. They don't worry enough." As far as their own lives are concerned, they have everything that they desire except good health. "I'd like to have my health back."

As the end of their lives approaches, Mr. and Mrs. Janousek wish to be left alone to enjoy rest, sleep, and peace.

The old days were full of work and hardships, but at any rate the people who lived about them had the same philosophy as they. Everyone wanted to work and to save money. They spent as little as possible. They were so filled with the idea of building that they could not enjoy the results of their efforts. The new generation is more concerned with enjoyment than with work, and this distresses the older people.

Most of the older people of Milligan live much as do these five. Their lives differ greatly from those of the young. Life lies before the young, behind the old. The young seek enjoyment, the old repose. The old were brought up in one culture, the young in another. It is inevitable that many of the activities in which the young engage should be displeasing to their elders.

Attitudes Toward Behavior of Young People

Although the children of Milligan have been brought up in the environment produced by their parents, they have not been brought up in a way that is completely satisfactory to their elders. The question, "What changes ought to be made in the behavior of the young people?" was asked nearly all the individuals who lived in Milligan. Some 617 different answers were given.

While the great majority of all generations believed that some changes should be made in the behavior of the young, there was a tendency for more of the first and second generations to find fault with the young than those who belong to the third. Seventy-four per cent of the members of the first generation thought that some changes should be made; 73 per cent of the members of the second generation thought likewise, whereas, but 64 per cent of the third generation thought that some changes should be made. Some such result should be expected in view of the large number of older people in the first and second generations. About one-fourth of all those who were asked this question replied that they did not believe any changes need be made. "Our young people are as good as any young people anywhere."

However, about three-fourths of all the Czech inhabitants of Milligan believed that some change should be made and 483 different suggestions were offered by 386 persons. In general, the main criticism was that the young people were enjoying themselves too much. Of the 483 answers, 105 suggested that liquor be taken away from the young or that they be encouraged to drink less. Eighty-three recommended that the young be deprived of automobiles. Fifty-five suggested that they run around less and stay at home more. Fifty-four recommended that they attend fewer dances, movies, and entertainments. A somewhat smaller number, 34, believed that the young people were too extravagant. One elderly grandmother, aged seventy-five, complained very much about the extravagance of the young. She advised the investigator to "save and save and save." She pointed out that the older people had lived very frugal lives and had saved considerable money, but that the young people were engaged in spending it as fast as they could. "What will become of them when all the money will be gone?" Some 25 individuals believed that the young people did not work enough. "When I was young I couldn't go chasing around all over the country. I had to stay home and work from sunrise to sunset." Twenty-four individuals believed that the young people were not deferential enough to their elders; the young people did not respect and obey their parents. Twenty-one complained that the young people smoked too much and at too early an age. An even dozen would allow the young people to go out in the evening, but insisted that they should come home at an earlier hour. Some 30 other suggestions were offered. In no case were there more than six individuals who agreed on any one of these. Some of the miscellaneous answers included statements such as the following:

"They organize clubs and elevate themselves. Then they feel that they are better than we are." "The girls should have more self-respect and should be more modest. They should dress up more." "They use awful language." "They drive carelessly and recklessly through the town." "They are boisterous and wild and vulgar." "They pet too much." "They go to school too long. They ought to quit school earlier and work on the farm." "The school doesn't discipline them." "They should go to church more." "They should be taught right from wrong. Some don't seem to know the difference."

In their study of Middletown the Lynds found that one complaint elders made against the behavior of the young was that the young people coupled off too much, that they did not go around in crowds as they did when they were young. Four individuals in Milligan made this criticism of the young. This particular criticism represented less than one per cent of the total number of answers. This would seem to indicate either that there is no great tendency on the part of the young people to pair off together or that the practice is not condemned by the community. Perhaps the first of these reasons is the correct one. While it is quite true that the automobile has made it possible for the young people to go off in couples to the neighboring towns to attend dances or entertainments, it is still quite common for them to go to dances and entertainments in groups rather than in pairs. There are still many entertainments and parties given in the homes. At the dances there is often a tendency on the part of the girls to stay in one end of the hall and the boys in the other. It is infrequent at a dance for a boy and girl to come together and dance with each other throughout the evening.

Non-Czechs in the Milligan community gave replies similar to those of the Czechs. The complaint made by the largest number was that the young people were too wild and lacked refinement. Only three believed that the young people drank too much. There was but one of the 50 non-Czechs who answered this question who believed that the young people were not sufficiently Americanized.

Are the changes which have been suggested unique to Milligan, or are they the sort that would be suggested in almost any community in America? Do they give evidence of a great gulf between parents and children, a gulf which is caused by the fact that the parents were brought up in the culture of the old world and the children in that of the new? How does the relationship between parents and children in Milligan differ from that to be found in an immigrant community in an American city?

Immigrant Youth and Age in the City

In most immigrant communities the break between the old world and the new appears more strongly in the relationship between parents and children than it does in any other aspect of the community life. Many studies which have been made of immigrant communities in large cities seem to prove that there is a higher rate of delinquency among the children of immigrants than among the children of the native born. The fact that the father was born in Europe and then migrated to America is believed to be the main reason for the delinquency of the children.[1] While this factor is important, there are other conditions which account for the greater delinquency of second-generation children.

Among the young people of Milligan there is very little delinquency or anti-social behavior. The process of Americanization has gone on at a slower rate and the young people do not feel that they differ greatly from the old. In the city the difference between the immigrant and the rest of the

---

[1] J. M. Reinhardt, and G. R. Davies, *Principles and Methods of Sociology* (New York, 1932), pp. 218–244.

community is very striking, and produces a defence reaction
on his part. He retires to the immigrant community where
he lives and in which he may speak his native language and
adhere to his native folkways. The great, bustling city over-
whelms him; the contrasts of wealth and poverty discourage
him. For years and years he struggles to save money and to
improve his status within the immigrant community. When
he thinks of the more fortunate people in the city who speak
the English language fluently he develops an inferiority feeling. This inferiority feeling is expressed in one respect by a
rigid adherence to the culture of the old world. He does not
wish to change and resists all efforts to change him. His
children, on the other hand, go to the public school where
they soon learn the English language, adopt American clothing and customs, and lose whatever they may have brought
with them from the old world. Within the family there thus
develops a great gulf between the older and the younger
members. The children feel ashamed of the parents and develop an inferiority feeling when they come in contact with
other children who do not have the handicap of a foreign-
born father and mother. Two factions are formed, one tend-
ing to pull the family back toward the old world, the other
trying to break away from the claims of the past and to
achieve a satisfactory status in the present surroundings.
Parents complain bitterly when the children do not use the
one language which they know and will not observe the moral
and religious customs which they brought with them to the
new world. The tensions which develop are not conducive
to the development of normal personalities on the part of
either the parents or the children. Youth and age find it
difficult to live together under most circumstances. How much
more difficult it is when not a generation but centuries separate the old and the young. This tragic process of adjustment
has produced many problems which society finds difficult to
solve.

Immigrant Youth and Age in the Country

Young people in Milligan do not feel themselves to be
centuries removed from their parents. The Milligan community has been rather isolated from the rest of the world. It is
composed almost entirely of Czech immigrants and their descendants. The individuals living within the community follow agriculture or depend upon it indirectly for their livelihood. There are no outside groups or classes which look down
with contempt upon the inhabitants of Milligan. Rather do

the Czech inhabitants of Milligan feel themselves to be somewhat superior to those who do not speak the Czech language. Those non-Czechs who have come to Milligan must conform to the attitudes and opinions of the Czechs if they are to secure a livelihood. Nearly all the customers of those who own stores are Czech people. Because of all these facts, the first-generation Czechs who live in Milligan have not developed an inferiority feeling. They are among their own people and but seldom see any others. The great world beyond the horizon comes to them refracted through the pages of the newspaper or magazine. These media do not examine the community with a critical eye. They try to sell, and in order to sell they must please. Hence, if anything, the Czech assumes a slight air of superiority.

Where there is no active opposition to the new-comer, the new-comer is quite willing to change. The first-generation Czech in Milligan may never learn the English language, but he does absorb a great deal of the culture of America without being conscious that he is doing so. Human nature cannot be changed by a frontal attack upon it, but can be influenced if the individual is not aware that a change is contemplated and being made.

Slow unconscious change in the nature of an individual such as occurs among the first-generation Czechs in Milligan tends to develop entirely new attitudes. The change may be slow, but it is sure. The past fades away and remains nothing but a beautiful dream.

In pioneer days the struggle with the soil was a very difficult task. During the course of this struggle the thoughts of the new-comer turned constantly homeward. Now, however, that the land is producing its harvest, that a new community has been built, the old world has lost its allure and the promise of the future can be fulfilled only in the new. The Milligan community represents in a sense the kind of community which those who dwell in it wish to live in, since they helped to make it. It is one in which they feel at home, one which they do not wish to leave. There is a striking difference, thus, between the first-generation immigrant in the city and the first-generation immigrant in the country. W. I. Thomas has pointed out that a city immigrant in America lives neither in the old world nor in the new, but in a third world, a world often of maladjustment and suffering.[2] The immigrant on the farm also lives in a third world, but not one of maladjustment or of suffering; rather it is a world which expresses his

---

[2] W. I. Thomas and Florian Znaniecki, *The Polish Peasant in Europe and America* (New York. 1918).

deepest wishes and his most profound beliefs. The making of the world lay in his own hands. The outside world has had but little influence upon him. He makes his own decisions, he selects his own way of life and lives it.

So much for the members of the first generation. What of the children? Children are usually pretty much what the homes make them. If the home is one in which there are few tensions, one in which a normal child life may be lived, the children are likely to be well adjusted to the community in which they live. The homes of Milligan are for the most part normal homes. There is no great gulf between the parents and children. The break between the generations is always less in the country than it is in the city. Hence, if anything, the gulf between the parents and children of the Czech part of the population of Milligan is considerably less than would be found between the parents and children of an American family in a great city. The old people do not wish to return to the old world from which they came. They have not needed to develop a romantic and illusory picture of the past as a defence reaction to the troublous realities of the present. They like Milligan. They wish to remain there for the rest of their lives. Some changes they would approve, but many they would not. They are normal individuals, well adjusted to their environment. The environment which the elders have created and which they approve is the one which has created the children.

This does not mean that the children resemble the elders in every respect. The replies given above intimate that the inhabitants of Milligan have many criticisms to make of the behavior of the young. However, the standards by which the young are judged are the standards which have been developed in the new world rather than those which were carried over from the old. Few, indeed, of the inhabitants of Milligan desire to make good Czechs of American citizens. Few of the non-Czechs complain that the Czechs are poor Americans. Not many of the people of Milligan really know what life in Bohemia is like.

Elders of all times have complained that young people enjoy themselves too much, or would if given an opportunity. Children are less repressed in America than they were in Bohemia. However, the greater freedom which children enjoy today has come pretty largely in the years since the first settlers came to the Milligan community. Even in Bohemia today children are much less repressed than they were fifty years ago. Hence, the complaint that youth is too free is made by old people everywhere. Czechs and non-Czechs alike found criticisms to make of the young, although the Czechs were a little harsher in their judgment.

Thus, few of the difficulties which arise between old and young are due to the fact that there is a great gulf caused by the fact that the old were educated in the old world traditions. Opinions in respect to the behavior of youth such as were found in Milligan might be found anywhere in America. The difficulties which arise between youth and age in immigrant communities located in American cities are due as much, perhaps, to the fact that the immigrants come from the country to the city as that they come from one national culture to another. The Czechs of Milligan are immune to many of the problems which confront immigrants in cities. Their lives are more tranquil; the control over their destinies is more completely in their own hands.[3] This tranquillity is reflected in the relationships established between youth and age.

---

[3] For an analysis of the difference between city and country see R. M. MacIver, *Society, Its Structure and Changes* (New York, 1931), Chapter XIX.

CHAPTER IX

THE SOCIAL ROUND

A Dance in Milligan Thirty Years Ago

All afternoon the members of the United Daughters of Bohemia have been busy at home preparing the food for the lodge dance tonight. After dinner they come to the hall bearing great quantities of wienies, rolls, and "koláce" which they deposit on shelves in the kitchen. The fragrant aroma of coffee soon fills the air. The bartender attaches a new keg of beer to his taps.

Everything is now in readiness, and the crowds begin to arrive. The families come in a body, bringing everyone from the oldest member to the smallest child. Some are fortunate enough to possess carriages, while others ride in their farm wagons.

A brass band has been hired for the occasion. The members are dressed in badly-fitting store clothing. They have brought with them some late Czech waltzes which they have been practicing for the last week.

The floor fills with couples who move to the slow and steady rhythm of the waltz. Many of the dancers are middle aged; a few have hair that is gray and bodies stiffened with age.

After the waltz a fast two-step is played. This is a number which some of the older women like to dance with members of their own sex. Fat, elderly women whirl around the hall, and woe unto the slender girls or small boys who come into contact with the gyrating couples on the floor. As likely as not they are bowled over and knocked into a corner.

While the dance is the central attraction, there are other features which are not to be despised. Between dances many of the people crowd into the kitchen to eat and to drink. No money is accepted by those who dispense the food. Tickets must be purchased from an elderly person who circulates through the crowd, crying out "Tickets, tickets." Almost always he is in evidence when one does not want to buy tickets, but when a small boy secures money from his father for the purchase of "koláce" and coffee, he is not to be found.

Coffee and "koláce" may be good enough for small boys and women, but for men there is another attraction which surpasses both of these. Out in the front room the long bar is lined with the men, while over its top passes a steady stream of glasses of beer. Many inches of waist-line present tonight owe their appearance to frequent attendance at the dances held in the community.

Children are very much in evidence at this gathering. Between dances they get out on the floor and play together. Hide and seek is a favorite game, and the forms of many of the elders offer a more than adequate protection for those who hide.

The clothing worn by the women is mainly home-made. The men are attired in business suits bought at the village store. Some of the women wear articles of clothing or jewelry which were made in Bohemia.

At midnight a long intermission is held. It is during this time that the desire of the people for food and beer is most completely satisfied. After the intermission the band continues playing, and the people go on dancing.

When the first gray streaks of dawn light the eastern sky the weary dancers decide that they have had enough, and start on their way homeward. The village newspaper is able to announce next week that the dance was a great success, and a large profit was made for the benefit of the lodge.

A Modern Dance in Milligan

This Saturday has been a hot day, and although it is nine o'clock in the evening, the temperature is still several degrees over the 100 mark. Inside the new auditorium the jazz orchestra is pouring forth its syncopated melody. On the drum is inscribed the name of the organization, "The Persians," while on the heads of the players are perched little red fezes. Lincoln is their home; the small towns of Nebraska constitute their playground. The young people of the community know a good orchestra when they hear one, and will not come if they are not provided with the best available.

On the floor of the hall a crowd of young folks sways to the blare of the saxophone and the strumming of the banjo. Slender young girls dressed in simple clothing glide gracefully across the floor in the arms of bronzed boys whose muscles still ache from the toil of the day. Only one young man wears a coat; all of the rest have their sleeves rolled up and their shirts open at the neck. It is hot work dancing in Milligan this night.

Most of the girls have bobbed hair, and a few have legs which are bare of stockings. The girl who wears the dress considered the prettiest by those attending the dance made it herself from a pattern of her own design. It is the custom in the village for the girls to make their own dresses, and the dancers believe that the results justify this practice.

When a dance is ended the girls usually return to one end of the hall, while the boys gather at the other. As the dance progresses some of the boys lose their bashfulness and follow their partners to the girl's side of the room. Here the young folks banter with each other, and make engagements for future dances. They meet and dance and meet again with the utmost informality. Tonight there are only three older people in the hall. These sit and watch the dancers, but do not take part in any of the activities. No chaperons are present, and youth is free to do as it will.

Toward midnight the orchestra announces that it needs a rest, but will play again later. In the basement of the hall, the coolest place in town, is a refreshment stand at which pop and hot dogs are sold. A few of the dancers betake themselves below, but the great majority rush out into the village street and crowd the three soda fountains. Busy clerks scoop up huge mountains of ice cream which go to cool the heated bodies of the perspiring youth before they return to dance away the evening.

These brief descriptions give some idea of changes which have occurred in one of the leisure-time activities of the people of Milligan. In so far as the dance is concerned, they have traveled far from the paths followed by their ancestors. The old world dances have disappeared. Where formerly no dance was a success without a "beseda," today few dances are given in which this old folk-dance is performed. The old people have forgotten it; the young have never learned it. Thirty years ago dancing was but one of the activities engaged in by those who gathered on a Saturday night at the old Central Hall. Many of those who came did not know how to dance. The food was as great an attraction as the floor, and the barroom was always filled with men, and sometimes women, who spent the long hours drinking, talking, and playing cards. Everyone came because there were activities in which all could engage.

Today a dance is a highly specialized activity. Only those who enjoy the modern dances attend. Its appeal is restricted mainly to the young. The character of the dancing has changed. The monotonous melodies to which the old folks turned round and round throughout the long winter nights have yielded to the staccato rhythm of jazz. The young have won the victory as far as dancing is concerned. Wherever the young are victorious the old world yields to the new.

Funerals

It may seem a little strange to include funerals in the social round. However, funerals are an important part of the social life of many of the people in Milligan. As one of the non-Czechs expressed it, "The people here like to go to funerals. More of them will attend a funeral than will attend a dance, even than will attend one of the old-time neighborhood dances. They will drive in from miles around. Often there will be a brass band to head the procession to the cemetery."

During the summer of 1930 a double funeral was held on a Sunday afternoon. Last rites were said over the bodies of one of the pioneers who had founded the town and a young man who had died of epilepsy. The ceremonies took place in the new town hall, as neither of those who had died had been affiliated with any church. The members of the fraternal lodges to which they had belonged conducted the services.

As the hour for the funeral approached the hall began to fill with silent men and women, some of whom brought their children with them. Most of the people were middle-aged or elderly. Many of the men had just come from the fields. Their faces were deeply lined and immobile; they moved with the slowness which is characteristic of the country man. The women were typical country housewives. They were bent and worn from the toil which had been their lot all the days of their life. Marriage to them had meant work from morning to night, the care of many children, the feeding of many mouths. Whatever desire they may have had to wear becoming clothing had long since died in the drab monotony of married life on the farm.

When all the mourners had come, the services began. They opened with a song, "Will There Be Any Stars in My Crown?" Then a duet offered, "God Will Take Care of You." The words of the songs were English. Next the gray-haired village banker in his dark suit and black bow tie faced the audience and delivered an eulogy of the dead. He spoke in his native tongue. At the close of his address a mixed quartet sang in Czech "Beautiful Isle of Somewhere." Then while the pianist played "Nearer My God to Thee," the relatives and friends filed past the caskets and bade farewell to the dead.

Before the services began everyone except the children had been silent. Now as the people left the hall everyone broke into conversation and spent some time visiting with neighbors. At the cemetery more songs were sung and another eulogy spoken over the open graves. When the services were over the mourners again broke up into little groups and discussed the many things which interested them.

A funeral is thus much more than a funeral. It is a gathering of the neighbors, an opportunity for the renewal of friendships. It is also a place where religious emotions may find expression. Most of the people in Milligan do not belong to any church, and relatively few of them attend church on Sundays. However, the emotions which are associated with the church find expression at the funeral. The songs which are sung are those which have given consolation to church-goers wherever man believes in God. Neighbor meets neighbor and feels better at the thought that life is still to be found in the world.

Clubs

"I don't like Milligan and I never did. I've always wanted to get away but I've not been able to do so yet. The people here are not very sociable. They have too many clubs. Unless you belong to one you are out of things. Sometimes two or three women will organize a club that really is not a club. I don't like to belong to clubs and so I stay at home."

People who form clubs are thus branded as unsociable by one of the non-Czechs, who has no use for such organizations. Anyone with such an attitude would be very unhappy in the average Czech community, for wherever Czechs establish themselves a great many different clubs and lodges are sure to be found.

Women's Clubs

"Mrs. C. Smrha entertained at a Christmas party Saturday, December 18. This was in a way a notable day, for the circle of friends had a christening and called themselves the Merry Wives. They didn't appropriate the entire title of Merry Wives of Windsor, nor did they care to plagiarize to the extent of calling themselves the Merry Wives of Milligan, but they just let it go at Merry Wives. The decorations in the home reflected the spirit of Christmas. The Christmas tree was there with the stockings hanging or dangling from the limbs—tree limbs, of course. These were filled with pop corn and candies and nuts and brought as much joy to the recipients as they might have done thirty or forty years ago—it being agreed and understood that time is not an essential matter in this write-up. In addition to the stockings the guests were the recipients of gifts from the hostess, into which they came into possession by following a string, one end of which was furnished them. While the luncheon was being prepared, books were passed, in which each guest was asked to compile an illustrated history of some member present. These

books proved to be when finished not only works of art but a collection of important historical data as well. It was late in the afternoon when the party was ready for lunch. It is generally agreed
that the afternoon was a splendid opening of the Christmas season
and left all full of the Christmas spirit."[1]

Thus was born another woman's club in Milligan. It
was a very informal organization, arising more or less spontaneously out of parties and entertainments given by its
members, and lasting for several years before its dissolution.
Its purpose was purely social. Its members included both
Czech and non-Czech women, but only those who were the
social leaders of Milligan.

Informal clubs such as the Merry Wives have been quite
common in Milligan's social history. They arise as congenial
individuals feel that their desire for good times can be best
realized by organizing a club, and disappear as the members
lose interest in a formal organization or as some of the members move away from the town.

A more formal and permanent organization is represented by the Woman's Community Club of Milligan. This
organization did not arise spontaneously, but was created at
the suggestion of the extension department of the University
of Nebraska. Its membership is open to all women in the
community. At its meetings projects suggested by the University are worked out.

"The ladies of the Milligan club held their first meeting Wednesday evening, January 27. There were twenty-seven ladies present.
Twenty-three enrolled for the work and goals which are to be accomplished. They had their first lesson, 'Let's look in the mirror,' and
made the color chart and read over the lesson, 'Making the most of
our individuality.' Then they went through the exercise of snow-
balling and closed with a song, 'Merrily row your boat.' "[2]

This year the project was "How to Dress Becomingly."
Project leaders met in the county seat and then returned to
each town in the county to conduct classes. At these classes
costumes were planned in accordance with instructions furnished the club.

In 1926 the club members turned their attention to a
study of the home.

"The regular monthly meeting of the Woman's Community Club
will be held at Z. C. B. J. hall Wednesday, November 10, at 7:30.
Please try to be on time.

"The first lesson on 'The Comfortable Home' will be given by our
capable leaders, Mrs. C. Smhra and Mrs. Frankforter.

[1] *Nebraska Signal*, December 23, 1920, p. 3.
[2] *Nebraska Signal*, February 4, 1926, p. 5.

"The club was represented at the state federation of women's clubs convention held in Lincoln October 27-8-9 by your president and a full report of convention proceedings and the entertainment provided by our Lincoln hostesses will be given at the meeting.

"Are you interested in your home? If so, be on hand at the meeting next Wednesday night and let's make this club season one of the most successful yet. Meet your friends and let's all enjoy the evening together."[3]

Between twenty and thirty women in Milligan attend meetings of the Woman's Community Club and work out the lessons furnished by the university. Occasionally the club is responsible for a party which touches the general social life of the community.

"The card party sponsored by the Milligan Woman's Club and held in Rut's pavilion last Wednesday evening proved to be an enjoyable event. About thirty tables were arranged in four rows, and couples were given a choice of playing five hundred, rummy, darda or taroky . . . At 12 o'clock the ladies served sandwiches, pickles, coffee and wafers."[4]

At the first meeting of the year some one of the men in the community may be given an opportunity to speak.

"A general meeting of the Milligan Woman's Club was held in the club room Thursday evening, November 10. Twenty-one members answered to roll call. Part of the evening was spent in conducting the business of the club, after which the members listened to an address by Gust E. Hohlfeld, a member of the high school faculty. It is always a pleasure to hear Mr. Hohlfeld, and his address on 'Woman's Influence' was especially pleasing to all who heard him."[5]

When the State University set out to improve the women of the state it did not rest content with telling them how to dress and how to make an attractive and comfortable home without spending much money. It realized that these were but externalities which may affect the life of the mind, but only in an indirect way. To improve the mind directly it suggested the formation of study clubs and offered to send lessons monthly to interested groups. One such club was formed in Milligan. It was not considered an independent organization, but rather was regarded as a subdivision of the Milligan Woman's Community Club.

The meetings held during the course of this year included topics such as the following: "Favorite American Poems"; "Favorite American Story Tellers"; "Some Nebraska Birds and How to Know Them"; "Our National Parks"; "Home

[3] *Nebraska Signal*, November 4, 1926, p. 5. The president this year was a non-Czech, but most of the members and one of the project leaders were Czechs. Interest in the club was quite general at this time.

[4] *Nebraska Signal*, May 19, 1927, p. 5.

[5] *Nebraska Signal*, November 17, 1927, p. 5.

Sanitation"; "Taking Drudgery out of Housekeeping," and "The Business Side of Housekeeping."

The lesson subject for January was "Nebraska," and included the following topics: "Song, 'Nebraska, My Native Land,'" "Names of Nebraska and Hall of Achievement," "Some Nebraska Facts," "Beauty of Nebraska Landscapes," "Nebraska Traditions," "A Tribute to Nebraska," "Song, 'My Nebraska,'" "Each paper showed much thoughtful preparation and every member was thoroughly convinced that Nebraska was the only state in which to live."[6]

Very few were the lessons which turned the attention of the club members to lands other than America or to times other than the recent past. One such dealt with the theatre. A history of the theatre was given, and a one-act play performed. Another meeting took up the subject of music. Sketches were given of the lives of Wagner, Mendelssohn, Donizetti, Chaminade, Sullivan, Chopin, Rachmaninov, and Dvorak. Selections from the works of each were played.

Other towns in the county have women's clubs which are active. In 1923 a county federation of women's clubs was formed. In 1928 the annual convention was held in Milligan. The program included vocal and piano solos, assembly singing, reading playlets and addresses. The addresses dealt with the subjects, "More Fun in the Home," "Religion in the Home," "Biennial and Federation News," and "Adult Educators." Each member brought sandwiches and a covered dish for luncheon.

Milligan has a number of other clubs for women, but the two discussed above are the most important from the point of view of social change. A Ladies Aid Society composed of women of the Methodist Church meets once monthly to sew and visit and discuss the ways in which the interests of the church may be advanced in Milligan. The Catholic Church has a similar society, called the Ladies Altar Society. These two societies bring to Milligan the viewpoints of some of the greater associations of the social system, and attempt to change its way of life. The main activity of each, however, is the bazaar which is held once a year and at which each society raises money for its respective church.

Children's Clubs

In the early days children of the Milligan community had to wait until they were grown before they could belong to clubs and lodges. Whatever spare time they had was

------

[6]*Nebraska Signal*, January 26, 1928, p. 5.

spent at the old swimming hole, or filled in with various forms of informal play. Too, they had but little leisure in the last decades of the past century. Men, women, and children spent most of their waking hours working. The newspaper of the time mentions dances, masquerades, and other activities, but carries no reference to clubs organized to pursue the interests of the young.

All of this has been changed during the past few years. Each issue of the county newspaper carries notices which describe activities of the numerous children's clubs. The school has been responsible for the formation of most of these club's. In connection with the agricultural courses 4-H clubs have been organized. Boys learn how to raise corn, pigs, cows, and other animals or plants found on the farm. A record is kept of the methods used and the amount of money spent. At the end of the season prizes are awarded to those who have been most successful, and exhibits are prepared for the county and state fairs. Girls likewise are members of these clubs. Most of the clubs to which girls belong are restricted to activities in which women only engage. In the club the girl learns sewing and cooking, and some of the intricacies of housekeeping. Milligan was very proud one year when two of the girls who belonged to the cooking club won the state championship in bread making.

Clubs to which boys belong are concerned mainly with activities which do not require many meetings of the entire group. However, girls' clubs do hold frequent meetings, and the activities carried on are often reported in the county newspaper.

"The Sunny Side cooks held their meeting at the home of Miss Sylvia Rischling Friday, July 25. Plans were made for attending the 4-H Club camp at Alexandria from August 4 to 7. Plans were made for a demonstration team at the county fair, demonstrating how to make muffins. . . .

"Sylvia showed us how to knead bread by pushing it once or twice and turn around quarter way and fold it over toward you. Anna Prokop told us how to take care of bread after it is cooled and ready to put away. The bread that the girls brought to the meeting was then judged. In the white bread Irma Havel had the best . . . In the whole wheat Marian Kassik had the best . . ."

"A delicious lunch was served . . ."[7]

Another of the clubs organized for girls is the Healthy Hustlers.

" 'We're Forever Growing Stronger,' is the song the Healthy Hustlers opened their last meeting with, and they really believe the hikes and exercises taken are making them stronger.

[7] *Nebraska Signal*, August 7, 1930, p. 5.

"A hike has been planned for Thursday, August 5. The groups will walk to Placek's creek and there have lunch before walking back home.

"Some plans were discussed for the county fair. By the next meeting everyone must have a health poster made. These will be brought to the meeting and the best ones selected to send to the fair. Rose Placek and Arline Bors will be the demonstration team. The topic of their demonstration has not been selected.

"A part of the fourth lesson was read and exercises for the feet taken. Some of these proved to be quite difficult."[8]

Children's clubs have a practical purpose, and the programs are prepared by outside associations. The walls of the community are being broken down, and the lives of the children are being changed by outside influences. The children who belong to the clubs are setting their feet on other paths than those which were trod by their fathers.

Fraternal Lodges

It is said that when Greek meets Greek nowadays they start a restaurant. Some maintain that when Czech meets Czech they start an argument, but this would· soon end if they had no organization in which to continue it. Inevitably the argument would lead to the formation of a lodge, in which they could argue to their heart's content.

Whether this is true or not, Czech communities have always been places in which lodges abound. The number of lodges found in Milligan has not changed appreciably in the last thirty years, fluctuating between ten and twelve, including both men's and women's lodges. Most of the organizations were founded in the decade between 1890 and 1900. The first lodge was established in 1888, and was a local of the C. S. P. S. (Bohemian-Slavonian Benevolent Union). This was followed in the 90's by three American fraternal societies, A. O. U. W., M. W. of A., and W. O. W. Today the societies are about equally divided between Czech and American lodges.

A great deal of the social life of Milligan centers about the activities of the fraternal lodges. The lodge serves both as a medium whereby the normal social life of the community finds expression and as an escape mechanism whereby its members may flee temporarily from their everyday life.[9] On lodge night the members leave the home circle with its familiarity and monotony, gather at the hall and engage in rituals and ceremonies which carry them away from modern America

---

[8]*Nebraska Signal*, August 7, 1930, p. 5.

[9]For the latter aspect see Charles Merz, *The Great American Band-Wagon*, Chapter III.

into an esoteric world. On initiation nights especially does the member find an opportunity to take part in experiences which are beyond the ordinary.

"The Modern Woodmen lodge of Milligan is growing right along in membership and has nearly 100 members now. Lately there have been several members taken in . . . The night these four were initiated it took six men to hold the goat as the boys, one by one, mounted him. Frank Vavra, Joe Rohla, and Rudolph Motis were the honorable committee that had charge of the goat that night, and they had stuffed him full of oats, oil cake and Hi-Hi bitters, and when he started around the room he was a holy terror. The boys hung on for their lives. Delaney gave up all hope of ever seeing the livery barn again; Mengler felt that some one else beside him would be selling farm machinery this spring; Hanus thought he had made his last harness, and Rozanek never hoped to see his farm again. But they were all rescued before being killed and each one grinned and said he was glad he was alive."[10]

Women as well as men find that lodge activities satisfy certain of their needs and desires. The lodge is regarded as a most important element in the lives of many Czech women. They will work long hours and make many sacrifices for the lodge. The following account of the installation of a chapter of the Pythian Sisters gives an idea of the values gained from lodge membership.

"Last Wednesday afternoon at 1:30 in Central Hall in Milligan there gathered a group of ladies who were interested in being instructed in the work of the Pythian Sisters.

"Grand Chief Olson gave the fundamental principles of the order, explaining the meaning of same. The password was taken from all the visiting members . . .

"Election of officers was one of harmony, an interested group of officers being elected and installed. (These consisted of a past chief, sitting past chief, M. E. C., excellent senior, excellent junior, manager, H. of R. and C., M. of F., protector, outer guard, three trustees, press correspondent, a representative, to the grand lodge and an alternate.)

"Friendship Temple No. 20 was the name and number chosen by the sisters. Meetings were to be held twice a month. Motion was made to adjourn until 7:30 in the evening. Some time was spent in meeting the visiting sisters and brothers, including thirty-five from York and seven from Crete and some from Hastings, who had come to assist in the work.

"All sisters, visiting sisters and brothers went to the spacious and open doors of Sister Marie Bors' beautiful home, where the Milligan sisters had prepared a delicious two-course covered dinner. The large dining room was very pretty with the well-filled table ready to give such good service to so many hungry folks; the eats were certainly good and were relished by everyone.

"The meeting was again called to order by the Grand Chief, after which the York Temple took charge of the meeting, conducting

10 *Nebraska Signal*, March 22, 1901, p. 7.   Quoted from *The Milligan Times*.

it in ritualistic form. . . . Sister Rose Placek was given the initiatory work, which was well given by the officers and degree staff of the York Temple. . . . A flower march was had and a nice collection was received to start a fund for the sick and shut-ins. A generous payment of dues was a good start toward a prosperous financial condition of the temple.

"Most Excellent Chief Sister Marie Bors presented Grand Chief Sister Olson and G. M. of R. and C. each with an appropriate framed motto, expressing their true friendship and love. These will be prized by the two sisters. It was indeed a surprise to receive such tokens of appreciation, but we will long cherish the memory of the time spent with these sisters. The meeting was then closed until the next meeting, after which kolace and hot coffee were served. The visitors expressed a wish to come to Milligan again and invited the local members to their temples."[11]

In addition to the direct participation of the members in the ritualistic work of the lodge and the social hour which follows, the society performs other functions in the community. In the course of each year the lodge gives dances and masquerades to raise money. In some instances it is instrumental in developing dramatic talent, producing plays from time to time. When a Czech lodge puts on a play it is usually given in the Czech language, and this helps to preserve the language in the community.

In recent times the lodges which serve Milligan have passed through a difficult era. The fundamental difficulty has been that the insurance which they offered was not based on sound actuarial practices. As long as the fraternal societies were new, the members young, and a large number of new members were added each year, it did not matter much what premiums were charged. As time went on the earlier enthusiasm faded somewhat, the members grew older and died in great numbers, and the number of new members added each year decreased steadily. As the organization saw its assets melting away it was forced to raise its premiums until they became nearly prohibitive. This was especially hard on the old members, many of whom are now old men and women who cannot pay the new premium rates and have been forced to drop out. This situation has created a great deal of bitterness among the older people of the Milligan community.

Czech lodges have fared better than have the American lodges, and are still adding members to their local chapters. From time to time the county newspaper contains articles in which attention is called to the activities of the lodges.

"As a result of a campaign for members which has been carried on by the local Z. C. B. J. lodges under the leadership of Josef Drtina, an organizer sent out by national headquarters, a large class was

[11] *Nebraska Signal*, April 4, 1929, p. 5.

initiated at a public ceremony at the hall of Joseph Jicha. Of these, thirty-six were taken into the adult classes and forty into the juvenile classes. There are probably about ten more who made application but some of these had not completed their examinations while others were unable to present themselves for initiation.

"Considerable interest in Z. C. B. J. matters is being taken at this time in view of the quintennial convention which will be held at St. Paul, Minn., next summer. At the last convention in Omaha. the organization voted to issue policies payable in twenty years and also endowment policies payable at the age of seventy. A new life table was also adopted based on the N. F. C. (National Fraternal Congress) table. There still remain, however, matters to be adjusted dealing with the old members and it is this in particular in which the membership is now interested."[12]

It is not hard to find the reasons for the greater success of the Czech fraternal societies. The American societies were in a much worse condition financially and have had to raise their rates to a much higher figure. Again, some of the early organizers of the Z. C. B. J. lodge live in Milligan. The village doctor is the medical adviser of the national organization. The banker is very influential in the national affairs of the lodge. The most recent chapter of the Z. C. B. J. is designed for the young, and conducts its meetings in the English language. Finally, the membership is restricted to Czechs, and since over ninety per cent of the members of the community are Czech, the Czech lodges would offer a greater appeal.

While they do offer a greater appeal to the Czechs of Milligan today, they nevertheless are confronted with problems on a national scale which may cause them difficulties in the future. In cities the young are being absorbed by the general life of America, and seek fulfillment of their lives in other associations which do not restrict their membership to individuals of one nationality. In some localities non-Czech husbands or wives of members are allowed to join. This is the beginning of a change in the character of the organization. If it restricts its membership to Czechs alone, the group from which it draws its members will diminish with the years. If it admits non-Czechs it will no longer serve as an agency for preserving Czech culture in America.

Czech fraternal societies in the past have had an ambitious program and have tried to pursue a great many interests. The leaders who founded them spent their early years in the villages of Bohemia, and they carried with them into the new world the pattern of life which they had known in the old. In a highly complex society the most efficient associations are those which restrict their activities to one interest or to a few related interests. Czech fraternal societies have tried to include within their activities too much of the life of their members, and hence find themselves today trying to pursue interests which are often unrelated. Some individuals today perhaps would like to preserve Czech culture in America, but would rather take out their insurance in a company which specializes in insurance. They may have only a little faith in fraternal insurance, but much sympathy with the social program of the lodge. Until the society defines its aims more clearly and restricts its activities to the pursuit of related interests it will not develop the unified and coherent program which is essential to the success of any association existing in a highly differentiated society. The Czech fraternal society is successful in Milligan today because the society in which the people live is not highly differentiated and the mental patterns of the people are nearer to those of the old world than would be the case in a more highly complex society. But even here the process of differentiation is going on and has already made its influence felt.

The Sokols

Since its establishment in 1894 the Tel. Jed. Sokol local in Milligan has passed through many ups and downs. In its early years it was a strong organization. At this time there were many arrivals from Bohemia. These individuals had been members of the organization in Europe, and it was but natural for them to take an interest in it in America. "It (Sokol Organization) was established in Prague, Bohemia, in 1862, at a time when the nation was awakening from a lethargy of two hundred years of repression of the language and national feeling . . . With the birth of this society or order a new national program was born. Equality, harmony, fraternity! A healthy mind in a healthy body! These were its aims. The object was dual: physical training for the body, national or patriotic training for the mind. The order grew and prospered and has always played an important part in the affairs of the nation. Lodges or clubs were formed in this country soon after the first immigrants settled here."[13] It is the only order in this country that had its inception in Bohemia. Its activities are open to both men and women. In America it has been the strongest association among the Czech people, with local units in nearly every Czech community. National tournaments, usually held in Chicago, bring

13 Rose Rosicky, *A History of Czechs in Nebraska* (Omaha, 1929), pp. 352-353.

together participants from every part of America in which Czechs are to be found.

During its early days the Milligan Sokol Organization took part not only in the state tournaments, but also in the national tournaments, which were usually held in Chicago. The following news item illustrates the interest displayed:

"Ben Smrha arrived home Thursday afternoon from Chicago, where he has been for nearly two months studying and practicing the new system of gymnastics arranged for use in various Tel. Jed. Sokol (Bohemian lodges) over the country. He passed examination in the highest class and has his diploma."[14]

In Milligan the Sokols did not at any time have a hall of their own, but used halls owned by other lodges. During the course of the winter the main event of the social season is the masquerade ball. One such is discussed in the local newspaper:

"The T. J. Sokol's masquerade ball turned out pretty well regardless of the storm which occurred in the evening.[15] There was a very large crowd present and everyone seemed to have a good time. The masks were numerous and some of the finest ever seen."[16]

In recent years the Sokol organization has had its ups and downs. On the whole there is less and less attention being paid to its activities. Interest in the Sokols revives from time to time, but it is never sustained. The last such revival began in 1925.

"Twenty years ago and more the Sokols were one of the liveliest organizations here. Classes in physical training met regularly and delegates were sent to all tournaments. Of late years the organization has dwindled down, some of the active ones having gone beyond the river and others having moved away or grown too old for the strenuous exertions to which the Sokol is put. There was also a strong girls' class and while they did not become active at any time in going through the physical exercises, they were active socially and were the sponsors of many pleasant events.

"In the past few years, the Sokols have been taking a new lease on life, several organizations having been formed in various parts of the state. Not to be left behind, Milligan formed an organization last Tuesday evening, Frank Chmelik, who came here direct from Czechoslovakia three years ago, spent a week here looking over the ground and holding classes at the school gymnasium. As a result of this, a meeting was called for Tuesday evening at the Z. C. B. J. Hall

14 *Nebraska Signal*, September 1, 1899, p. 2. Quoted from the *Milligan Journal.*

15 Until very recent times the possibility of meeting expenses at all public gatherings in Milligan was dependent on the weather. Muddy roads kept not only the farmers, but also residents of neighboring towns at home. Time and again the village newspaper ascribes the lack of success of social events to the fact that it rained. The "large crowd," reported was usually present only in the editor's imagination. Today one gravel road leads into Milligan, but all of the side roads are still unsurfaced. Expenses are made today regardless of weather, but a large profit can be made only if the sky is clear.

16 *Nebraska Signal*, March 1, 1901, p. 2. Quoted from the *Milligan Journal.*

and an organization was formed. An admission fee of $5 was agreed
upon and the further payment of yearly dues of $5.

"A boys' class will work every Monday afternoon and Monday evening and a girls' class Tuesday afternoon and evening. . . . Mr.
Chmelik is expected to return here in about five weeks and with his help
there can be no doubt that the organization will grow. Those desir-
ing to become charter members were given an opportunity to do so
until December 8. When the next state tournament is held it is
to be hoped that Milligan will be there to develop some prize winners
among the youngsters who are taking hold of the work with a vim."[17]

Under the leadership of the recently imported Mr. Chmelik, interest in the work grew and the organization expanded.
In May of 1926 it was ready to show the homefolks what
had been accomplished.

"Friday evening the local Sokols gave an entertainment to a large
audience of their friends, showing the progress the young turners had
made in their drills and calisthenics and also for the purpose of getting ready for the state meet at Omaha on the Sunday following.
About eighty-five or ninety boys and girls took part, and all did their
work creditably and to the satisfaction of those present.

"First about thirty of the little girls gave a ball drill which was
very well done, not many of the girls missing the balls while performing. Next they were joined by nearly as many boys and gave
a combined calisthenics drill, the girls drilling a different combination than the boys. Then followed the high school girls, who gave a
very fine drill with rings and then the large boys' class gave a drill
that had a difficult movement to execute at almost every change.

"Then came the apparatus work, the large girls performing on
the double bars and the larger boys on the vaulting horse and the
double bars. Simon Rokusek of Omaha, president of the western
division of the Sokols, installed our club into the national organization and was followed by Stanley Serpan, also of Omaha, who gave
a short talk on the purpose of the organization. . . . Frank Chmelik
of Prague, Czechoslovakia . . . has been training the various
western clubs for more than a year. Mr. Chmelik is going home
the coming month to be present at the eighth convention of all the
Sokols which is held every sixth year, at which time more than 30,000
men and women are to drill and perform. (Several of the local people)
are sailing with him to take in this great meet and to visit their old
homes."[18]

This year marked one of the high points of the revival of
the Sokol movement in Milligan. On the Sunday following
the exhibition described above, the state tournament was held
in Omaha. Many of the inhabitants of Milligan were present.
A special train which started in Milligan and picked up a
number of delegates from along the way was filled with several hundred contestants and spectators before it arrived
in Omaha. Of the affair the local correspondent wrote:

[17] *Nebraska Signal*, November 26, 1925, p. 5.
[18] *Nebraska Signal*, May 27, 1926, p. 5.

"The exhibition at the auditorium was a revelation to those who witnessed it. The auditorium hall was full. The exercises came in a methodical and orderly manner and the drills were given with precision. The Milligan contingent took part in the various classes and did exceptionally well; the girls' drill with rings being particularly good. The day was a good day throughout and the crowd got home about midnight, tired but happy."[19]

The Sokol spirit was in the air at this time, and another tournament was held in August at Wilbur, a neighboring town. A crowd estimated at 5,000 people saw Milligan teams win several prizes. At Thanksgiving a Sokol benefit was given for the purpose of helping the lodge in Omaha construct a new hall. More than $200 were realized; "the community responded very liberally in furnishing food and other things to make the day a success."[20]

In 1927 another tournament was held in Omaha. The Milligan lodge was growing in numbers, and planning to meet some of the objections of the younger members.

"By another year we hope to have our Sokol organization in shape so that they will be able to take part in tournaments outside the state. In 1929 a national meet will be held in Chicago and by that time we should have a class ready to compete at this tournament. The activities of the Sokols are being modernized by the addition of such games as basketball and baseball, making the work more appealing to the average American boy. During the coming season it is expected to lay the foundations for a Sokol basketball team which will be in condition to take part in contests the following year."[21]

Milligan sent to this tournament five classes which included fourteen young women, eleven young men and seven little girls. This year the local group was not very successful, two individual prizes only being won, one by a boy and one by a girl.

Interest in the Sokols had been growing steadily in Milligan for two or three years. It was now believed that the time was ripe for Milligan to entertain on its own account. In June, 1928, the state tournament was held in Milligan. Many were the preparations which had to be made.

"By Sunday all preparations will have been made to put on the big Sokol doings and take care of the crowd which is expected here for that day. Places to lodge the more than one hundred participants who will take part in the exercises have been found without difficulty.

"The ladies have had charge of the problem of feeding not only the participants but the several thousand guests as well. They have the really big job of the whole undertaking, but they have taken hold of the work with a will and no one who comes here will need to go

[19] *Nebraska Signal*, May 27, 1926, p. 5.
[20] *Nebraska Signal*, December 2, 1926, p. 5.
[21] *Nebraska Signal*, May 26, 1927, p. 5.

hungry, if he has the nominal price charged. Music for the occasion will be furnished by the band from Cuba, Kan., and it is expected that most of Cuba will be here. The exercises will begin promptly at 1 o'clock. After the Sokol drill a ball game will be played between Milligan and Carleton. This is not a part of the Sokol program and regular admission will be charged to witness the ball game. Altogether, this is expected to be the biggest day in Milligan's history."[22]

The tournament was a great success from all points of view. The Milligan participants won their share of prizes. One of those who played a conspicuous part was a non-Czech boy who lived in Milligan.

This event marked the zenith of the Sokol revival in Milligan. The next year classes were held, and the district trainer spent some time with the local organization perfecting their work. The earlier enthusiasm was beginning to fade, and the classes to dwindle in numbers. In the summer of 1930 only eight men in the village and four who lived on farms mentioned the Sokol organization as one of the societies to which they belonged. Eleven children mentioned that they attended the weekly Sokol gymnastic meetings. Ten of these came from first- and one from second-generation homes. None of the children living on farms displayed any interest in Sokol affairs. In one household three reported that they used to go, but none went now. One said, "Everyone went at first; nobody goes now."

It would appear as though the Sokol organization in Milligan is doomed to extinction in time. There may be sporadic revivals, which will usually coincide with the arrival of an enthusiastic trainer from Bohemia, but the interest will not be sustained. The school provides the children with an opportunity to engage in interesting competitive games, which they may select according to their own desires. Calisthenics and apparatus work may be interesting to some, but do not provide direct and immediate competition. The Sokol movement aims at an all-round development; it can realize its ends in a simple society where no other associations exist to serve special interests. Again, in Bohemia the Sokol organization was the focal point of the patriotic movement; all who loved Bohemia belonged to it. In America the young know not the land of their fathers; this motive for becoming members does not exist for them. So passes the old to be replaced by the new.[23]

---

[22] *Nebraska Signal*, June 14, 1928, p. 5.

[23] These conclusions apply to Milligan. They raise similar questions in regard to the future of the Sokol movement elsewhere in the United States. In the cities there is a larger Czech population on which to draw, and also in recent times the bulk of the Czech immigration into the United States has settled in urban communities. Therefore, it would be natural to expect

Dramatic Societies

While the dramatic society may not be indispensable to the establishment of a Czech community, yet such a community is not long in existence before at least one such association is formed. Two years after Milligan was founded the newspaper recorded the success of a Czech play. "The Bohemian home talent rendered last Saturday 'Trasák a Basa,' at the Kotas opera house in a very creditable manner."[24]

Among few people is there to be found the interest in drama that is present in Czech communities. The Russian, Evreinoff, mentions the people of his native land as being preeminently actors,[25] and perhaps it is the Slav element in the Czech which makes him love the stage and all that goes with it. Throughout its history Milligan has been treated to liberal doses of the Czech drama, and the end is not yet.

In the early days of the community Czech plays were the only ones offered to the people. Today a traveling company of players brings English plays to the community, but the largest crowds are found at the Czech dramas. There are several dramatic societies in the village, the most recent of which consists almost exclusively of young people, who present Czech plays in a way which is acceptable to the older people. Their first play was a great success.

"One of the biggest crowds for a home talent play that Milligan has had for many years turned out Thanksgiving night to witness the play of the Ceska Lipa Dramatic Club, recently organized by Father Biskup, to witness their presentation of 'Zmatek nad Zmatek.' This play is a very clever comedy and for a Thanksgiving play when a good laugh is needed to help in the digestion of a Thanksgiving dinner it proved to be a very happy selection, because it kept the crowd in an uproar sufficient to digest several dinners.

"Father Biskup selected and coached the play and its presentation showed his mastery of the art. The ticket receipts were better than $300 and everybody who was there seemed to agree that it was money well earned. It is hoped that Father Biskup will take time to help put on other plays by this group in the playing season."[26]

urban lodges to continue active for a longer period of time than will lodges in country districts, where few recent immigrants have settled. Again urban lodges have proved more adaptable to the trend of the times. Thus Cleveland and New York lodges have purchased summer camps, where boys and girls are sent each summer. Competitive games are engaged in, and leagues are formed in which the teams play. In spite of these attempts, the membership does not increase but rather falls off. The members lost are usually the more progressive, the better educated; those who are in the professions or in business. These move to sections of the city far from the hall, and live their lives in other social groups. Potential leaders are lost to the organization. The real crisis will not come until its present leaders, who are mostly foreign-born, will have passed away.

[24] *Nebraska Signal*, October 24, 1889, p. 1.
[25] Nicolas Evreinoff, *The Theatre in Life* (New York, 1927).
[26] *Nebraska Signal*, December 5, 1929, p. 5.

This play was such a success that it attracted the attention of neighboring Czech towns. The next month the club journeyed to Bee, Nebraska, where it presented the same production. Dramatic clubs in other towns often come to Milligan to present the plays on which they have worked.

"The Dramatic Club of Bruno presented a play at Jicha's hall Saturday evening, which drew a good audience and which was thoroughly enjoyed by all who saw it. The play was an operetta depicting the merry life of the old country mill and depicting also, of course, the pathos which comes with every story where love has a part.

". . . The Simen orchestra of Brainard was also here and furnished music for the dance which followed the play. The visit of the club was thoroughly appreciated by followers of home talent plays, and it is hoped that their visit may be repeated when they have another play prepared."[27]

After the play a dance is usually held. The proceeds of the dance are generally donated to one of the lodges or to the local unit of the Sokols.

Once or twice a year a company of professional actors comes to Milligan and presents Czech dramas.

"Don't fail to see the Cesko-American Narodni Divadlo given here on the evening of July 6 and 7 under the management of Joseph R. Krejci of Chicago. Among their plays are 'Baby Mine,' 'Where the Meadow Lark Sings,' 'The Twins,' and 'Merry War.' This is an unusual treat for all lovers of this sort of entertainment and all who attend are assured of an evening well spent."[28]

While the Czech drama is more popular in Milligan than the English, road companies which tour the small towns of Nebraska do not despair of getting an audience. The article which announced the coming of one of those companies is indicative of the type of entertainment which such organizations offer to the community.

"The Hazel McOwen Stock Company, which plays the Central Hall and Opera House at Milligan, Nebraska, on the night of December 14, is reputed to be the best organization of its kind on the road today. The company has formed a circle of towns including Wilber, Geneva, Edgar, Clay Center, Sutton, Exeter, and Crete. playing each one on the same night every two weeks. At present there are a couple of nights to fill in, and the company is playing Milligan with the intention of including it in the circle permanently should the patronage warrant.

"The best of reports have been given from Geneva and Wilber, where the company has already played. Their plays are of the finest and produced by an A-1 company of ladies and gentlemen, each one a star in his respective line.

²⁷Nebraska Signal, February 13, 1930, p. 5.
²⁸Nebraska Signal, June 29, 1922, p. 5.

"The play that has been chosen for Milligan is one of the most beautiful bills ever written, entitled, 'The Girl From Out Yonder,' a comedy-drama in four acts.   The highest class of vaudeville is introduced between each act, including the Hazel McOwen quartette of excellent singers which is well worth the price of admission alone, singing in harmony the very latest and best ballads and numbers.   By all means come out and see this excellent company and be assured of seeing a good high-class show played by a real company once every two weeks."[29]

On the opening night the attendance was very small. The unfavorable weather was blamed, and the company was persuaded to return again in two weeks.   By this time playing in Milligan had become a habit with the company, and for several seasons the village remained on the circle.   The town never became very enthusiastic over the productions, and always remained the poorest theatre town in which the company played.

As far as the drama is concerned, the people are much more interested in Czech plays than in English productions. The type of drama offered by the Czech societies is generally superior to that offered by the English-speaking companies.   The acting, although amateur, is rather good, and the actors have many friends and relatives in the audience. The money is usually devoted to some worthy cause.   The lines may be followed even by those who do not understand the Czech language very well.   The Czech drama, therefore, is one of the most important links which the people have with the old world.

Summary

A number of ways in which Milligan has organized its leisure time have now been surveyed.   As in previous chapters we find some evidence of persistence and some of change. Organized leisure, however, shows more evidence of change than do other aspects of the community life.   Outside associations can affect Milligan most readily through the organizations which have been formed in the community.   Some of these associations wish to change the life of the community, and try to introduce ideas which will produce this effect. Thus the woman's club draws its inspiration from the university, with its "boiler-plate" programs designed for an American audience.

Other organizations, such as Czech lodges and the Sokols, try to preserve the culture of the old world.   The Sokols have a much more difficult time than do the lodges in holding the attention of the individuals in the community. The strength of the Sokols lies in the young, and the young are fast becoming Americanized. The sport activities which the Sokols foster do not fit into the athletic program of the youth of Milligan.

With the lodges the case is somewhat different. The grandfathers and grandmothers of the community can and do work to make the lodge a success. The older members of the village are conservative and try to preserve the culture of the old world. Tremendous effort on their part keeps the lodges going more or less in the old ways. They cannot, however, stop the change which is going on in the community, and are forced to organize English-speaking lodges to attract the young. Thus, while the lodge at present does represent a conservative force in the life of the community and is much more effective in its work than is an organization like the Sokols, the day is not far distant when the lodge itself must change to conform to the new ideas now entering the community.

Of all the elements found in the organized leisure of the community, the one which is most effective in the preservation of the old-world culture is the Czech-speaking drama. Czech dramas draw crowded houses, and the life of the old world is re-created for the benefit of the citizens of Milligan. However, it is difficult to determine whether these dramas are successful because they are Czech or because they are produced by amateurs who live in the community. Again, there are still found in the community many old people who possess but an imperfect understanding of the English language. Nearly all of the members of the second and third generations understand the Czech language. Hence a larger audience can be secured if a play is given in the Czech language.

It may be concluded, therefore, that that part of Milligan's leisure time which is organized is rather highly susceptible to the forces which produce change.

CHAPTER X

INFORMAL HOURS

"Friday evening, December 7, cars from all directions were headed toward the home of Ignac Sebesta and his wife. They came from the south and the north, the east and the west, and swooped down on the Sebesta home like a flock of crows, except that they were more welcome than crows and also, unlike crows, they brought their commissary stores right with them instead of mooching off of their prey. The affair was arranged and planned as a surprise and the host and hostess carried out their part of the secret as well as could be expected under the circumstances.

"The occasion was the birthday of Mrs. Sebesta and also her nameday, which was generally observed on the following day. The home was hardly large enough to take care of the company which gathered, but, remembering the old adage that where there is a will there's always a way, when the folks got ready to dance, they just took hold of the stove and carried it out, then took out a door or two and there was room enough to swing 'em around until their heads whirled. Ach and Slepicka and Kucera furnished most of the music, that is, the instrumental music. The vocal music was furnished by the whole company and they sang until the very roof raised and the foundations shook. It was a jolly and a merry crowd out for a good time and they had it.

"At the proper time, the lunch baskets were brought out. In these were provisions enough to feed a whole regiment and they were things, too, that tasted mighty good and stuck to the ribs with firm tenacity. It was long after midnight before the company broke up and then they broke up by ones and twos, many of them lingering until much later."[1]

About fifteen families were present at this neighborhood party. Hardly a week passes but that one or more parties of this kind are held somewhere in the community. Much of the leisure time of Milligan is organized, but the greater part of it escapes organization. Listening to the radio, neighborhood visiting, reading, stripping feathers, hunting and fishing, picnics, playing games—both indoors and out—and sitting on the benches on Main Street are a few of the ways in which the inhabitants of Milligan re-create themselves in their spare time.

Leisure-Time Interests

Some of the activities in which the people engage go back to the old world, whereas others are to be found only in the new. "Main street visiting" is probably common to both lands but it represents perhaps more persistence than change. In the village of Bohemia people live "all together," and

[1]*Nebraska Signal,* December 13, 1923, p. 5.

Czechs in the new world have not seen fit to shut themselves away from their neighbors. During the long summer days those who have retired sit on the benches and dream of the past. In the evening the soft-drink parlors are filled with visitors, while the benches are occupied by both young and old. On open nights the village radio blares forth its program. Life goes on much as it did on the long single street of the villages of Bohemia. The monotony is broken by an occasional fight or drunken brawl, or perhaps by the retailing of some choice bit of gossip.

An insight into the way people spend their leisure may be gained by asking them what they would do with an extra hour a day. This question was answered by about 500 of the Czech residents of the Milligan community. About 10 per cent felt that they would put in their time working. Most of them would work about the house or yard, but 10 of these would have preferred some type of income-producing work. Better care of their cows would have occupied the leisure hour of two individuals, while one poor overworked wife would have taken advantage of the extra time to finish up the ironing and washing of her large household.

At the opposite extreme stand, or rather lie, those who feel they need rest and relaxation. This group, some 159, was about three times as large as the first. Eighty-eight wanted to rest, while 44 wanted to go the whole way and sleep. Farmers find life much harder than do those who live in the city; about two-thirds of those who desired rest and sleep lived in the country. Eleven of the individuals who replied wanted to sit uptown and look at the world.

Recreation of some sort or another attracted another fairly large group of 109 individuals. The largest number, 22, would have enjoyed play of some kind. Some would have liked to act in amateur theatricals or sing in a chorus, while others would have liked to play baseball or some other athletic game. The next largest number, 21, would have taken the family car and visited their neighbors. Fourteen would have gone fishing. Twelve would have been delighted if they might have had the chance to play music, or sing at home. Other activities, favored in each case by less than 10 individuals, consisted of such things as the following: Going swimming, walking in the country, riding in the car, listening to radio in the home, going to lodge entertainments, sitting uptown and listening to radio, playing cards, and being happy. The indoor sport favored by one young girl was that of killing flies.

A group of women, 41 in number, favored a form of fancy work as a leisure-time occupation. Sewing, knitting, crocheting, and embroidery work would occupy the nimble fingers of this group. Women of all ages and all three generations were interested in these household tasks.

But few of the activities discussed thus far have as their objective the education of the individual. However, there were in the Milligan community 10 individuals who wished to pursue a definite course of study, while a dozen others expressed the desire to read literature which would have educational value. A few of the first-generation women who could not speak English would have enjoyed studying English in their spare time, while a few of the men who were in business or a trade would have taken advantage of the extra hour to learn more about their work. Three of the individuals would rather have preferred to give to others the fruits of their knowledge by writing letters to newspapers. All of these people were older members of the first generation. The average Czech newspaper in America is filled with the voluntary contributions of such as these.

The remaining individuals, slightly less than one-third of the total, indicated preference for reading as a leisure-time occupation. The proportions are about the same in each of the three generations.

Thus would the Czechs of Milligan spend their time if they had more leisure. Many of them do spend whatever leisure they have in the ways indicated, while some no doubt seldom do the things they desire to do. Reading, sleep and rest, recreation, and work are the most important activities in which they would like to engage. Commercialized amusement possesses little appeal. Not one of the individuals expressed a desire to attend the movies. Only two wanted to listen to the radio, although many of them no doubt do listen to it in their spare time.

Newspapers

A number of the earlier immigrants to America were newspaper editors who had been banished from Bohemia because of their opposition to the Austrian state. As more Czechs came to America these men founded newspapers and carried on their activities in this country. Chicago soon became the center of Czech life in America, and several influential papers were founded there. These are read by Czech people all over the United States. Most of the Czech newspapers were rather liberal in their viewpoint, and appealed mainly to those who joined the free-thinking movement. In St. Louis, however, the Czech Catholics founded a newspaper known as *Hlas* (Voice) which is still rather widely read by Czech Catholics.

In 1871 Edward Rosewater, editor and publisher of the *Omaha Bee*, established the *Pokrok Zapadu* in that city, the main purpose of which was to induce immigrants to settle in Nebraska. Later a number of other Bohemian newspapers were established there. These flourished as long as a steady stream of immigrants flowed into Nebraska. However, recently the Czech papers in Nebraska have fallen upon rather difficult times. The only newspaper which still survives is the *Narodni Pokrok* (National Progress).

Only one newspaper published in Czechoslovakia is received in the community. *Hlasatel*, the Czech newspaper with the largest circulation in Milligan, is a liberal organ published in Chicago. The next most influential of the newspapers is the *Narodni Pokrok* of Omaha. A Catholic newspaper, *Hlas*, comes next in importance. As far as the formation of public opinion through the medium of the Czech press is concerned, the newspapers published in Chicago have a much greater influence than does the newspaper published in Omaha. The *Narodni Pokrok* is more or less a newspaper which records the weekly events transpiring in the various Czech settlements scattered about Nebraska. It is a neighborhood newspaper rather than one which emphasizes general news or which tries to influence public opinion through its editorial column. During the early days of Czech migration to Nebraska there was a very vigorous community life, and each group was very much interested in the life of the various other settlements. As the small self-contained communities are broken down by the improvement of transportation facilities the vigor of the community life diminishes and there is less demand for a neighborhood newspaper. The general news today may be secured from English newspapers, which have a wider circulation in Milligan than do the Czech newspapers. Thus the only Czech newspaper which has a very great appeal to the residents of Milligan is one with a vigorous editorial column. The Catholic and liberal newspapers advocate definite policies and those living in the community who favor these policies continue their subscriptions.

Czech newspapers have 98 subscribers among the 177 Czech families interviewed in the Milligan community, whereas English newspapers have 222, of whom 72 take only the Sunday issue. Eighty-seven of the 98 subscribers to Czech newspapers are members of the first generation. Only 11 belong to the second generation. The conclusion may fairly be drawn, therefore, that as members of the first generation die off the subscribers to the Czech newspapers will gradually fall away until they finally cease to exist.   The conviction that this will be the case becomes all the stronger when it is realized that some of the members of the second generation living in Milligan were brought up in the Nebraska of fifty years ago.   Most of the 11 second-generation subscribers belong to the group of older persons who never really learned to speak English.   It is reasonable to conclude, therefore, that Czech newspapers are virtually non-existent in the homes of the younger individuals of the second generation.

In time to come the only newspapers which will be circulated in the Milligan community will be those printed in the English language.   Whereas, there are only 10 Czech newspapers which enter Milligan homes interviewed, there are 19 English news-papers.   The one which has the largest circulation is the county newspaper, the *Nebraska Signal*, with 67 subscribers.   While this local newspaper has more subscribers than any other, the combined circulation of newspapers published in Lincoln and Omaha exceeds that of the *Nebraska Signal*.   Of the newspapers published in Lincoln the *State Journal* has 40 subscribers; the *Daily Star* 28.   The two newspapers published in Omaha have a total of 31 subscribers of which the *World Herald* has 22, the *Omaha Bee* nine.   Thus there are 101 subscribers to Lincoln and Omaha newspapers.   Of newspapers published in other cities the *Kansas City Star* is the most influential with 24 subscribers.   The *Denver Weekly Post* has five subscribers.   The cashier of the bank takes the *Commercial Journal*.   This accounts for all the newspapers outside the state except the *Valerian* published in Montana, and the *Chicago Tribune*, which has one daily and four Sunday subscribers.   The community in which the former newspaper is published is one of those to which the surplus population of Milligan migrates.   The other English newspapers taken by the inhabitants of Milligan interviewed consist either of newspapers published in surrounding towns or farm papers published in Lincoln or Omaha.   Of 222 subscribers to English newspapers 98 belong to the first generation; 124 to the second.

An analysis of the newspapers found in the homes of Milligan reveals a significant fact.   The Czech newspapers which are most influential are those which are published in distant cities. The English newspapers which are most influential are those published in nearby cities.   Thus as the circulation of the Czech newspapers drops off and the circulation of the English newspapers increases, local or state newspapers will determine the public opinion of the community.

Some of the non-Czechs are no further removed from the old world than are the second-generation Czechs.   None of them, however, subscribes to newspapers published in the language of their fathers or mothers.   Thirty-seven out of 50 non-Czechs interviewed subscribe to newspapers including the *State Journal*, the *Nebraska Signal*, a few Omaha, Lincoln, and Denver papers, as well as local papers from surrounding towns. There is little difference between the Czech and non-Czech groups as far as subscriptions to English newspapers are concerned.

A total of 150 copies of English daily newspapers are received by the 177 Czech households visited. Twenty-eight of the households received no newspaper. This average is somewhat below that of another Nebraska community, Gibbon, studied by the Bureau of Agricultural Economics in co-operation with the University of Nebraska. In this community an average of one daily newspaper was received in each home.[2] However, there are 98 subscriptions to Czech newspapers in the Czech group, none of which appears daily. Perhaps if these publications were included the average in the group would be somewhat higher than that in Gibbon.

Magazines

There were 659 subscriptions to 131 different magazines in the 177 Czech households interviewed. One hundred and forty-four homes received one or more magazines while only 33 received none. Of these latter homes, 24 were first-generation homes, of which all except two were found in the village of Milligan itself. Nine were second-generation homes, of which seven were in Milligan, two on the farm. Most of these first-generation homes consisted of older people, generally widows and widowers or old bachelors who are not much interested in reading but pass away their days sitting on the benches on Main Street or playing cards at Jicha's hall. The farm homes were much more likely to take magazines. In the first place, the farm inhabitants, on the average, are considerably younger than the town inhabitants. In the second place nearly all of the farmers subscribe to one or more agricultural magazines which contain articles useful to them in their work.

One-half of the 144 households with subscriptions were first generation and one-half second. Among them were 81 separate subscriptions to 10 Czech magazines. Sixty-four of these were subscriptions given by first-generation people, 17 by second generation. Of the 64 first-generation subscriptions 44 came from the village and 20 from the farms, while eight of the second-generation subscriptions came from the village and nine from the farms. It would thus appear that a large proportion of the first-generation homes and but few of the second subscribe to Czech magazines. This condition is similar to that found in the case of

² *Reading Matter in Nebraska Farm Homes*, United States Department of Agriculture, Washington, D. C., 1924.

newspaper circulation.   As the old die off the subscription lists of Czech newspapers and magazines will diminish.

English magazines are becoming increasingly important in the lives of the people of Milligan.   Fourteen of the 121 English magazines subscribed to by the Czechs visited have 10 or more subscriptions in the Milligan district.   Heading the list is the *Nebraska Farmer* with 61 subscribers.   Following this comes *Household* (45), *Woman's World* (39), *Capper's Farmer* (32), *Country Home* (22), *Successful Farming* (22), *McCall's* (21), *Farm Journal* (21), *Capper's Weekly* (17), *Poultry Journal* (16), *Country Gentleman* (15), *Needle Craft* (15), *Pathfinder* (12), *The American* (10).   Eight of the 14 magazines are farm publications, four are publications for women, and two, *The Pathfinder* and *The American*, are magazines of a more general nature.   The remainder run about as do the first 14.   A great many of them are magazines which would interest the farmer or the housewife, some are lodge publications, and a few are publications of professional or business interest, such as the *American Medical Journal*, *The American Dental Association Journal*, *The Grocery Magazine*, *National Petroleum News*, *The Banker's Association Journal*, and *American Builder*.   A few of the magazines are denominational publications, as *Catholic Extension*, *Sacred Heart Messenger*, and *St. Anthony's Messenger*.   Some of the more general magazines taken were *The Literary Digest* (seven), *Popular Mechanics* (seven), *National Geographic* (six), *Pictorial Review* (five), *Saturday Evening Post* (five), *True Story* (three), *Cosmopolitan* (two), *Western Stories* (two), *Liberty* (two), *Travel* (two), *World's Work* (one), *Good Housekeeping* (one), *Delineator* (one), *True Detective* (one), *Master Detective* (one), *Collier's* (one), *Photoplay* (one).   A few of the sportsmen in the community receive magazines devoted to sports, such as *Hunting and Fishing*.   *Etude* has one subscriber.   Two of the homes visited subscribe to the *National Republic*.   Subscriptions to this magazine were urged by one of the teachers in the local high school.

The magazine reading of the people of Milligan is not of very high literary standard.   The postmistress reports that in the whole community there is not a single subscriber to *Harper's*, *Scribner's*, or *The Atlantic Monthly*.   Whatever educational value the magazines possess is confined almost entirely to farming or some business or profession pursued by the reader.   There is no subscriber in Milligan to the more liberal magazines, such as the *New Republic* or the *Nation*.   This is a rather surprising fact when one considers that the more liberal or more radical Czech magazines and newspapers possess a great appeal.   One is forced to the conclusion that the selection of magazines reflects high pressure salesmanship rather than any intelligent selection on the part of the readers.

It has already been pointed out that 144 Czech homes in Milligan received one or more magazines, whereas 33 received none. The 144 homes received a total of 81 Czech and 578 English magazines. On the average, therefore, slightly less than one Czech magazine is received in every two of the homes, whereas the average circulation of English magazines per home is 3.2. In first-generation homes Czech magazines average slightly less than one per home, whereas the English average about 2.5 per home. Only 17 Czech magazines find their way into some of the 76 second-generation homes, while each of these homes on the average subscribes to 4.2 English magazines. About two-thirds of the total number of Czech magazines are received by people living within the village, and one-third by farmers. However, the proportion of first-generation people in the village is greater than that in the country. It is among these homes that the Czech magazines are circulated.

There is thus a greater number of magazines taken by second-generation homes and nearly all of these are printed in the English language.

Of the 18 non-Czech families visited, 12 lived in the village, six on the farms. Among the non-Czechs as among the Czechs the most popular magazine was the *Nebraska Farmer* with one subscriber in the village and five on the farms. The next most popular magazine was *Woman's World* with five subscribers, all living in the village. *Household Magazine* had three subscribers, one in the village, and two on the farms. Seven other magazines had as many as two subscribers. These included the *National Geographic, True Story, Liberty, Catholic Mission, Good Housekeeping, The American* and *Capper's Weekly.* Thirty-five other magazines had one subscriber in the Milligan district. Non-Czechs subscribed to the same sort of magazines as did the Czechs. Six were professional and business magazines, seven were agricultural publications, five were women's magazines, five were religious or fraternal publications.

Non-Czech magazine subscriptions totaled 64, an average of 3.5 per household. This average does not differ greatly from that of the Czech homes.

Books

Milligan as yet can boast of no library, hence all the reading which penetrates into the community must be bought by the inhabitants or borrowed from friends. The daily or weekly newspapers, and the weekly and monthly magazines find their way into most of the homes in the community. It is very infrequently, however, that any inhabitant of Milligan buys a book. Of 177 Czech homes interviewed only 44 reported the purchase of one or more books in the course of the past year. Twenty-three of these were from first-generation families and 21 from second. Since there was a total of 101 first- and 76 second-generation families in the group, a slightly greater per cent of the latter bought books. However, the 23 first-generation families bought 196 books, while the 21 from the second generation bought only 154. Although Czech books are more difficult to obtain than English books, over half of the books bought by first-generation families were in Czech. Many of the books that were bought by the inhabitants were sold by book agents who came to the community. Nearly all these agents sold English books.

Of the 44 families buying books, 28 lived in the village and 16 on the farms. The percentage is about the same in each case.

Within the past year a total of 350 books were bought by the 44 families. One hundred and three of these were Czech books, 247 were English. First-generation families bought 101 of the Czech books, whereas second-generation families bought but two. Ninety-five of the English books were bought by first-generation families, 152 by second-generation families. It is rather interesting also to note that of the 101 Czech books bought by first-generation families, 95 were bought by families living in Milligan; but six were bought by families living on the farm. Thus it would appear that as far as Czech books are concerned, their circulation is confined pretty largely to older members of the first generation who live in the village. There is practically no market for Czech books among the second-generation families. Here again evidence is secured with respect to present and future trends in the Milligan community. As the older members of the first generation die off there will be fewer and fewer Czech books sold. Within a few decades there will be almost no Czech newspapers, magazines, or books read in the community.

A very large majority of the 350 books bought in the past year were novels. The Czech books consisted of 79 novels, 21 historical works, two educational books, and one volume entitled, *A National Cemetery Memorial.* It is significant that no children's books are included in the list. The English books bought were 147 novels, 36 books for children, 8 historical works, 19 books of educational value, 10 volumes of theology purchased by the priest, and 27 miscellaneous books including biographies, encyclopedias, song, psychology, and auto-repair books, and a set of volumes on nursing.

Among the non-Czechs in Milligan there is about the same degree of interest in books as is found among the Czechs. Seven of the 12 non-Czech families who live in Milligan and five of the six non-Czech farm families bought no books. Six families bought a total of 62 books of which 30 consisted of encyclopedia volumes. The tastes of the non-Czechs, therefore, did not differ very much from those of the Czechs. The influence of the book agent is seen in the volumes of encyclopedia bought.

In the preceding paragraphs an analysis was made of the books purchased during the past year by each household. In addition to this each member of the household was asked to tell whether or not he had read any books in the same period. A total of 505 Czechs replied. Two hundred and sixty-one of them replied that they had read one or more books, whereas 244 replied that they had read no books. First-generation replies showed 37 who had read one or more books, 103 who had read none. Second-generation replies showed that 136 had read one or more and that 118 had read none. Third-generation replies showed 77 affirmative and 23 negative. Thus as one goes from one generation to the next a larger proportion is found to be reading books.

Book readers succeeded in reading 342 books, 261 of which were English and 81 Czech. The subjects were similar to those of the books bought during the year.

Those who read Czech or English books average 1.3 per person. This average may not seem to be very high, but when one considers the vast numbers of newspapers and magazines that descend upon Milligan weekly, it is surprising indeed that even one volume per person is read. Also, Milligan possesses no library. Whatever books the inhabitants read must be bought by them or borrowed from their neighbors.

Milligan is thus subjected to many influences from the outside world. Newspapers, magazines, and books circulate rather freely throughout the community. The books are read mainly for entertainment, whereas magazines are often concerned with vocational activities. In the reading matter of Milligan is reflected the change in the life of the community. At one time it would have been difficult to have secured any reading matter in English. Within a few years it will be difficult to find any coming to Milligan written in the Czech language. During the early days of the community's life a good deal of the literature was printed in Bohemia. Today almost the only reading matter printed in Bohemia consists of the Czech books that still find their way into the homes of the first generation.

Music

Milligan differs from many other Czech communities in America in that it has been unable to organize the musical interests of the community in recent years. In its early days Milligan boasted of a "silver cornet band," but strenuous efforts to revive this organization in the last few years have resulted in failure.   However, the failure is not due to lack of musicians. Among 508 Czechs, there were 148 who play one or more musical instruments.   There are fewer musicians among the first generation than among either of the others.   Fifteen of 140 first-generation people played musical instruments, 93 of 266 second generation, and 40 of 102 third-generation persons.   Of the 148 musicians, 84 were men and 64 were women.

Among the 19 musical instruments played the piano ranked first in number of performers, with 60.   Following came the accordion (39), violin (22), clarinet (10), cornet (10).   The other instruments were played by fewer than ten persons.   Seven boys played the saxophone.   As far as instruments played are concerned, there is strong evidence of the old world in the presence of the accordion.   However, this is usually a solo instrument, and the other instruments may be used to play the music of the new world as well as of the old.

Informal types of musical organizations are found among the young people.   Several of the boys practice together for a few nights and then play at dances held in the community. In one family the five sons have a jazz orchestra of their own. These organizations play popular music.   In immigrant settlements where music is organized on a community basis it is possible to preserve the music of the old world.   The fact that Milligan has not been able to develop a community orchestra or chorus means that the folk songs of Bohemia are not played very often. In order to listen to Bohemian music the inhabitants of Milligan must tune in their radios on a program broadcast from Hastings or Omaha.

Radio Programs

When the first settlers came to the Milligan community they found themselves to be quite isolated.   In the last few years the community has come into contact with life beyond its horizon in a variety of ways.   As long as the newspaper or the commercial traveler represented the main channels by which the world filtered into Milligan, the inhabitants had to make some effort to obtain news of the world.   Today, however, all day long and sometimes far into the night the radio blares forth its programs in many of the homes of Milligan, and the living room and the world have become one.

When one of the older Czech inhabitants of the community is asked what type of radio program he likes best, he usually replies, "I don't turn on the radio unless there is some Bohemian music coming in."   Five hundred and nine Czechs gave 559 answers to the question, "What radio programs do you prefer?"   Two hundred and fifty-five expressed a preference for Bohemian music as against only 90 who replied that they liked popular music better. Only three members of the first generation expressed a preference for jazz as against 93 who believed that Bohemian music was superior. In the second generation the majority in favor of Bohemian music was about two to one, whereas in the third generation there was a slight majority in favor of jazz.

There are, of course, relatively few programs which offer Bohemian music. Some of them come at hours when it is almost impossible for the inhabitants to listen. Many of them, however, love the Bohemian music so much that they are willing to get up at six o'clock in the morning in order to hear it.

Other types of programs, given first preference by relatively few inhabitants, such as speeches and lectures, talks and stories, news items, market reports, radio plays, athletic programs, household talks, and so forth, are tuned in occasionally. It is rather interesting that only two women in the community expressed a preference for "household talks." All of the other women undoubtedly felt that they had learned enough from their mothers, from courses taken at school, or from household magazines to enable them to run a house successfully. Only one farmer expressed an interest in farm programs. He listened to the market reports daily. The weather forecast was of interest to but two individuals in the community. Athletic programs appealed to three members of the third generation. One farmer enjoyed listening to programs broadcast by the university.

Of 509 Czechs who replied to this question there was but one who expressed a preference for church services broadcast over the radio. Those few inhabitants who are religious attend church services which are held on Sunday mornings in the Catholic Church or take part in the Sunday School activities in the Methodist Church. Those who do not go to church occupy themselves in other ways on Sunday mornings.

All of the answers discussed above indicate some preference on the part of the individuals concerned. Fifteen inhabitants, however, were not very critical with respect to the programs offered. "It's all the same to me"; "I like all programs"; "I turn the radio on in the morning and let it go all day," are some of the answers given by this group. Sixteen individuals replied that they had no radio and did not listen. Thirty-three replied that they either did not listen or paid no attention to it. One old person who lived in the village asked, "What is the radio?"

These answers give us some insight into the type of life lived by the inhabitants of Milligan. Goethe said, "Every Czech is born with a violin in his hand." The love of music which was a vital element in the community life of Bohemia persists very strongly in the new world. Popular modern music has won over a rather considerable number of the young people, but even among them the old-world music which delighted their forefathers still seems attractive when it comes in over the radio. To the people of Milligan the first function of the radio is to supply music and entertainment. The utilitarian uses to which it may be put are of little interest. Thus we may conclude that this newest contribution of the new world is used primarily to continue an interest that was predominant in the old world.

Among the non-Czechs as among the Czechs the most popular radio programs are those in which some form of music is offered. However, the type of music which is preferred differs somewhat from that which is liked by the Czechs. Popular or jazz music is preferred by the largest number. Sixteen preferred popular music, 11 preferred old-fashioned music, and an equal number preferred classical music. When asked whether they liked Czech music, 11 of the 50 who were questioned replied that they did. Symphony orchestras, pipe organs, vocal music, Irish music, semi-classical music, and old-fashioned hymns were preferred by several people in each case. Five replied that they liked any kind of music. "Amos and Andy" appealed to three of the individuals. Other types of programs which were enjoyed by one to four individuals in each case included lectures, radio plays or vaudeville, educational programs, political speeches, sporting events, and religious services. Three individuals liked all of the programs, two did not listen, and one had no radio.

If we compare the replies of the Czechs and the non-Czechs, the outstanding difference is the decided preference of the Czechs for Bohemian music. The non-Czechs are interested in a greater variety of programs, although music dominates their radio dials as it does those of the Czechs. There is a slightly greater interest in religious programs, but the housewives in each group displayed little interest in programs which would help them in their housework. Sporting events were of little interest to each group.

While some activities in which the community engages can and are modified considerably by associations and influences outside of Milligan, the type of music which is enjoyed is and has been in the past determined by the old world.

Whether this will be true in the future or not is difficult to say. Whether the radio will draw children away from the music of their fathers it is hard to determine. As far as the present is concerned, however, the radio has had little influence in modifying the likes and dislikes of the inhabitants of Milligan.

Movies

One should expect the movies to be an influence making for the adoption of American ways of life by the people of Milligan, for does not all the world enjoy America's favorite screen stars? Most of the movies which are shown in Milligan are typical Hollywood productions, and reflect the producer's conception of life in America. Occasionally, however, the village newspaper announces the presentation of movies which were made in Czechoslovakia, and which reflect the life with which the older members of the community were familiar in their youth.

"There may not be a Hollywood in Czechoslovakia, but the screen talent of Czechoslovakia is ambitious to have its product known the world over. The Czechoslovak is sentimental, talks with his face as well as with his hands and his whole body and uses all the devices with which he is endowed to give expression to what he has to say so that he ought to make a good movie actor. They are far behind us, however, in mechanics and this applies to the mechanics of making pictures as well as to mechanics in all other lines. The fact is that American films, like all things machine made, cannot be duplicated anywhere in the world.

"It is interesting to note the difference of interpretation of the Bohemian artist and our artists. The marked difference comes in the development of the climax and emphasizing salient features which lend themselves readily to effective display. The Czechoslovak films are interesting not only because of the contrast but because they are an accurate portrayal of manners and customs and scenes of Czechoslovakia, the directors apparently having more regard for truth and accuracy than for effect.

"Saturday, June 28, and Sunday, June 29, 'Billy and Dot,' and 'The Last Kiss,' both of them Czechoslovak films, will be shown at Central Hall."[3]

If the producers of Czechoslovak films had any hopes that they might find a ready market for their products in Milligan they were doomed to disappointment. These films were regarded more as a curiosity than as regular film diet. Perhaps once a year films do penetrate from the hinterland of Europe to the Nebraska prairie. When some important event such as a Sokol tournament occurs in Bohemia, films are usually made and sent to the United States. Pictures of the tourna-

---

[3]*Nebraska Signal*, June 26, 1924, p. 5.

ment held in 1920 were shown in Milligan several months after it was held.

Czech films are infrequent visitors to Milligan, while the Hollywood productions are seen several times weekly. Here the typical hero pursues a villain and rescues the heroine from his clutches. The effect of these films on Milligan is much the same as it is on any group in America. An article such as the following exemplifies the type of movie often shown at the theatre:

"The 'Sage Hen,' which will be shown at the Gem theatre Sunday, April 9, is a drama that goes straight to the mother heart of the world, being the poignant story of an outcast woman of the early West who was branded with the scarlet letter and turned out on the desert with her little son to die."[4]

Western movies are very popular in Milligan, as are magazines which feature western stories. The old west which the pioneers knew or dreamed about is more interesting to the people than is the Bohemia from which the old folks came. As a matter of fact, the old folks in the village are but little interested in movies. The attendance at each performance is made up almost entirely of children. And children like wildwest plays better than they do any other kind.

In most American cities today, all movie shows present "talkies." Milligan is not behind the general procession. Early in the spring of 1930 the talkies made their first appearance in Milligan.

"The Central theatre . . . has installed talkie equipment and gave its first public performance Saturday. . . . This equipment is being installed at an expense of about $2,000. It compares favorably with that of the smaller theatres in our neighboring towns."[5]

Although the management of the Central theatre was desirous of pleasing its patrons and was willing to spend quite a sum of money to give them better movies, the results which it obtained were not of the best, either as regards the quality of the presentations or in respect to the attendance at the performances. Patrons complained that they could not understand what was being said on the screen, and attendance, which had never been good, began to dwindle.

In the movie is seen one of the influences working for change in the community life. Czech films are not a success, and come but infrequently to Milligan. When they do come they do not pull the members of the community back toward the life of the past. They are regarded as curiosities, and the

[4] *Nebraska Signal*, April 6, 1922, p. 5.
[5] *Nebraska Signal*, March 20, 1930, p. 5.

life they present is foreign to that which is lived by Milligan. They mark the change, rather than slow it up. American films serve as an escape mechanism, especially for the young. They, too, present a life which is foreign to that which is lived by Milligan, but it is a life in which the inhabitants would feel more at home than they would in Europe. Indeed, there is still pretty much of the pioneer element left in the blood of the people. This finds a vicarious outlet in the movie and the magazine, but some of it is translated into real life rather than reel life. In Wyoming, in Montana, and in Canada are settlements founded by individuals who spent their early years in the Milligan community. Nearly all of the individuals who expressed a desire to travel wished to turn the nose of the Ford toward the setting sun. Europe does not interest them to any great extent, whereas beyond the great divide they expect to find the mystery and romance which cannot be found in the realities of present-day Milligan or in the memories of the old world.

The Chautauqua

During the days of the World War there was a great deal of interest in the Chautauqua in Milligan, but unfortunately the interest was not often apparent in the gate receipts. Nearly every year the individuals who signed the contract were forced to make up a deficit. Finally the sponsors rebelled, and for several years no Chautauqua has come to Milligan. The last one was held in 1925.

"Monday a number of business men signed a contract for a Chautauqua of four days to be put on some time during the month of August.
"Chautauquas have not been exactly what you might call a howling success before—except for the howling of those who have had the deficits to pay for, but that does not necessarily mean that they cannot be made so. They do bring to town a series of programs that is worth taking in."[6]

Early in August the Chautauqua came to Milligan. It had been planned to buy playground equipment with the profits from the Chautauqua. However, Milligan children had to do without their playground apparatus this year, for the Chautauqua ran true to form and showed a deficit.

So ended a heroic attempt to introduce "culture" into the community. Work and the weather usually cut down attendance. The entertainment and instruction offered were often not of the best. Many of the inhabitants of the com-

---

[6] *Nebraska Signal*, February 5, 1925, p. 5.

munity could not understand the speeches and plays. The Chautauqua is primarily an American institution, and its spirit is somewhat alien to that of the people of Milligan. The Chautauqua was introduced into Milligan as much because it stimulated business as because it educated and entertained. As long as business was improved, backers could be found. Recently, however, the business men have sought other and less expensive methods of stimulating business.

Summary

There is found an intermingling of old and new in the various ways the people of Milligan spend that part of their leisure time which escapes organization. In their parties and informal visits they play both Czech and American games. In their reading they are deserting the Czech language in favor of the English. In their radio programs they select those which remind them of the old world. The people sit uptown on the benches and talk away the days, much as they used to do along the village streets in Bohemia. While there is an intermingling of cultural elements, there is present today less of the old-world culture than was true thirty years ago. As the language is lost more of the old culture will disappear. However, the loss of cultural elements is gradual and involves but little conflict.

CHAPTER XI

COMMUNITY

On a drowsy Sunday afternoon Main Street in Milligan is devoid of all activity. A few of the older men sit at their usual places on the benches along the wide, sun-drenched avenue which is the pride of Milligan, and discuss the same interminable subjects which have occupied their attention in the past. Of the stores, the soft-drink parlors alone are open, and only the old regulars are found in them. Some of the houses of the village are crowded with visitors, but the noise from these houses is hardly heard on Main Street. An aviator passing through the blue heavens overhead would probably look down and remark, "Another one of those dead country towns." However, the pulse of Milligan's life does not always course as sluggishly as it does on this Sunday afternoon. As even the most humdrum of lives has its great moments, so too have the people of Milligan experienced moments when their lives were filled with intensity of emotion and moved by the desire to do great things.

In Milligan there is no lack of the booster spirit which is characteristic of American life in general. If there are no great things which the people can do, they are determined to do small things in a big way. On two occasions especially the town people scaled the highest heights of enthusiasm, and felt for a moment they had accomplished more than had ever been achieved by any people anywhere in the world. The coming of the purebred sire train was responsible for the first outburst; the building of the new auditorium for the second.

The Purebred Sire Train

It was in 1924 that the purebred sire train came to Milligan. The article in the county newspaper which describes the affair has a headline in large capital letters, "MILLIGAN'S BIG DAY." Subheads contain the words "A Tremendous Crowd, Great Enthusiasm and Remarkable Parade." An understanding of the great day is best obtained through the description of the town correspondent:

"The big day came Thursday, October 23, and 3,718 individuals passed through the train and viewed the exhibits. The afternoon was given over to the biggest and finest parade of floats ever seen in Fillmore County. Thirty-one floats of local business houses, local lodges, district schools, old-time farm implements, flail threshing, and retired farmers were in line.

"The Farmers & Merchants Bank float led the parade. It was prettily decorated, advertising over half a million dollars on deposit and saying that the local bank reflected the prosperity of the locality. Adolph Zeman had four International tractors in line advertising the fact that one can plow for gold by plowing deep. James Bors had a nicely-decorated Fordson tractor resembling a submarine. The Milligan Lumber Co. had a pretty bungalow with children playing in it and a decorated lawn.

"The Farmers Co-operative Co. had about twenty-four men pulling a loaded farm wagon. The men were in line pulling the rope. They kept going steadily forward even when others, appropriately placarded, were putting on the brakes, throwing brickbats at the wheels and otherwise trying to make progress more tedious. They well represented the idea that enough men must pull together to make the proper progress. Kassik & Sons had a well-decorated truck advertising their mill products and their elevator.

"All three local Western Bohemian Fraternal Association lodges had floats. The most elaborate of these was that of Lodge Rabi, which displayed a large emblem and a home fireside with the breadwinner absent and the widow and children receiving the benefits of fraternal insurance. They displayed the motto, 'Keep the Home Fires Burning.' Lodge Svatopluk Cech displayed an old-time Cech plow and depicted an event in Bohemian history. The ladies' lodge Cechie had a decorated car in which rode Mrs. Katherine Smrha, the oldest local member, together with the youngest members, little six-year-old Elenore Hrdy and others."[1]

Several of the district schools had floats depicting the value of education and the necessity of using purebred sires. The American Legion float won first prize.

"The finest float and the one receiving the first prize was the American Legion float. They had a truck decorated to resemble a hospital room. The truck driver was hidden under a piece of furniture. On a cot lay a stricken soldier who was attended by two beautiful nurses. No wonder he was stricken! The float was escorted by soldiers and sailors and had a most beautiful emblem worked out in corn and wheat. It was certainly a dandy float, and well deserved the prize.

"The old-time flail threshing was pictured by Mrs. Ignac Sebesta and Mrs. Vaclav Halama, Albert Frycek and Vaclav Svajgr, dressed in Bohemian national costume. Their float was prettily decorated and they made a pretty picture, threshing wheat, oats, and rye. Following this float was one decorated with farm products in which rode many retired farmers and their wives, sitting in rockers, some reading, others smoking and talking among themselves and having much enjoyment. They illustrated the fact that this territory is prosperous enough to retire its older members to comfort and rest. Their float bore the motto, 'We Have Earned Our Comfort.'"[2]

One of the floats was a take-off on the business men of the community.

"The surrounding farmers got up a float that was a joke on the business men. About twenty-five farmers decorated a float that was

1 *Nebraska Signal*, October 30, 1924, p. 1.
2 *Ibid*, p. 1.

escorted by four pretty clowns, while they themselves were decorated with scarfs across their noble chests, each with the name of the business man he burlesqued. The whole represented a session of the Chamber of Commerce. E. E. Slepicka represented Dr. Smrha as president of the chamber and he explained the meaning of the assembly. He was followed by Vaclav Ach, who has much forensic ability and who represented Charles Smrha. He read the minutes of the previous meeting. The motions that were made and the debate that followed were read out of the minutes and were most comical and entertaining."[3]

The parade was led by the local band. A number of notables gave speeches, and motion pictures were made to serve as a permanent record of the great occasion.

"The train visited thirty-one points in the state. At but one stop did the number of those passing through the train exceed that at Milligan and this was Broken Bow. Something over 4,000 people passed through the train there, so that Milligan lacked but few to be the top-notcher of the state. Had it not been for the fact that the train was in Geneva just two days before its stop at Milligan and for the further fact that the Bryan meeting at Geneva on the same day conflicted with the local affair, there is no doubt but that the Milligan crowd would have broken the record.

"The Milligan Chamber of Commerce is highly gratified over the result of the affair here. The co-operation of the surrounding school districts and the people in general was so generous and so wholehearted that they are encouraged to believe that nothing is impossible and are confident that the local spirit is of a nature to put anything across they put their hand to."[4]

It was indeed a day to be long remembered. Not all of the floats were relevant to the coming of the purebred sire train, but all of them called for creative expression on the part of the people. The inspiration for a number of the floats came from the old world, but the inspiration for the affair as a whole came entirely from the new.

After such a great outburst of enthusiasm, a respite was necessary. For several years the community rested on its laurels. The Sokol tournament held in Milligan in 1928 required much co-operation on the part of the people, but the occasion was not one which called forth the enthusiasm of the purebred sire day. However, while bazaars and tournaments were being put over by the people in a matter-of-fact way, an idea was germinating among them which was to arouse the community to a white heat again. The success of the purebred sire day gave them the confidence necessary to insure the solution of a problem which had long bothered them.

[3] *Nebraska Signal*, October 30, 1924, p. 1.
[4] *Ibid*, p. 1.

Building the New Auditorium

For some years Milligan had been in need of a new auditorium. The old hall had been built in the 1890's, and was very inadequate. In 1929 a campaign for funds was inaugurated and about $15,000 were raised. When bids were asked, the committee discovered that a suitable hall could not be built for less than $50,000. An appeal was made to the lodges to raise the necessary money. They put on an intensive drive for funds, and succeeded in raising an additional $10,000. The committee decided to start building the hall, relying upon the sale of $25,000 worth of bonds to complete the cost of the building.

It was not an easy task to sell the bonds, however. If the committee had waited until all the bonds had been sold, the auditorium would never have been built. Before the ground was broken for the new building the committee expressed its disappointment at its lack of success.

". . . the committee which undertook to raise money by volunteer subscriptions was very much surprised and disappointed in the raising of funds. With but a few exceptions the amount subscribed by different individuals was far below that which the committee expected. In a number of cases they came away empty-handed when they felt sure of a liberal donation.

"The difficulty seems to lie in the fact that the people who have means haven't the generous spirit and the people who have the generous spirit haven't the means. It is no small project that the community has undertaken and it will require the loosening of the purse strings more than the exercise of the vocal cords to put the project through."[5]

After the ground was broken the community took great interest in the construction of the building, and longed to see its completion. In November, 1929, the committee decided to issue the bonds, urging everybody to "Buy a Bond and By a Bond be Bound to Milligan." In this same month the necessity of completing a given piece of construction before freezing weather set in made it imperative for the men of the community to give of their muscles as well as of their money.

" 'Everybody works but father' is a thing of the past in the present day when necessity requires everybody working, including father. Friday the contractor at work on the community auditorium was particularly desirous of having as much concrete poured as possible for fear freezing weather might set in and seriously retard the progress of the work. He let his wants be known to Jim Charvat and Jim said to him, says he, 'I can get you all the men you want who will stay on the job until it is finished.'

[5] *Nebraska Signal*, October 17, 1929, p. 5.

"So Jim proceeded to spread the news that all able-bodied men were requested to be at the auditorium by 6:30 that evening and help pour concrete until the contractor hollered 'nuff.' About fifty fellows were on the job at the appointed time.

"It was a jolly crowd. Wheeling that wheelbarrow up a steep incline wasn't light work, either. Some of those wheelbarrows didn't seem to have the carburetor working right and some of them seemed to be running on flat tires, but the push behind them kept them going until the job was completed. The building of King Solomon's temple or the construction of the Chinese wall must have been some job, but when you get together a bunch of fellows who seem to have the spirit there just isn't anything that can't be accomplished."[6]

In April, 1930, a month before the auditorium was dedicated, the last of these bonds were sold. In many instances individuals borrowed money at a high rate of interest to buy bonds which gave a smaller return. When the bonds were all sold the local correspondent complimented the community on its achievement.

"The financing of this $50,000 project speaks volumes for this community. The past six months haven't been especially favorable for the raising of ready cash for the reason that prices of farm products have been unsatisfactory and farmers haven't been selling, but in spite of all this the money has been raised and we have witnessed another demonstration of what a community can do when a respectable number of people get behind a project and determine to stay with it until it is achieved."[7]

Each week the newspaper reported the progress which had been made during the previous week. As the building neared completion the committee was confronted with the problem of its dedication. Elaborate plans were made, and for three days Milligan gave itself up to rejoicing and congratulation.

"As originally planned, the dedication of the new auditorium comprised three days. It had not been planned, however, that they should be three hectic days. The plans and specifications called for three sunshiny days, but the committee had some misgivings about this and as a precaution invested in some rain insurance, and they surely had need of it. It rained Friday and it rained Saturday. It didn't rain Sunday, but that made no difference, because the roads couldn't have been any sloppier if it had rained for the last thirty days.

"But even the rain couldn't stop the fitting climax which had been planned for observing in a fitting manner the completion of so fine a project as the construction of this splendid public building. All of the programs were carried out as planned and while they were not witnessed by capacity houses, the attendance was such as to demonstrate conclusively that under favorable weather conditions the attendance would have been of such proportions as to have made it beyond all power to take care of the throngs. As it was, it was possible to handle the visitors satisfactorily and send them home with a desire to come again."[8]

[6] *Nebraska Signal*, November 21, 1929, p. 5.
[7] *Nebraska Signal*, April 17, 1930, p. 5.
[8] *Nebraska Signal*, May 1, 1930, p. 6.

On Friday the ceremonies opened with a concert and a dance. On Saturday afternoon the governor of the state and other notables gave addresses. Saturday evening a problem confronted the committee.

"Saturday evening was designated for the jazz dance. A ten-piece high-priced orchestra was engaged from Omaha for the occasion. At about 7:30 they called up from Seward that they were having trouble with one of their cars, but would send seven of their men on ahead and the rest would follow later, if possible. About an hour later they called again that they couldn't come at all. The dance committee sweated blood and oozed tears and almost swore. "They called up frantically everywhere they had ever heard of an orchestra being. They called up York, Clay Center, and Lincoln. They called Crete and Tobias, thinking dances there might have been called off and their orchestras be available. But to no avail. Something had to be done. So finally Jim Ach with his accordion and the help of his two sons and John Kucera took their places on the stage and substituted for Jimmy's Serenaders. Jim did a good job of it. That is, Jim Ach did. If the Omaha Jim with his serenaders had made half the effort to fulfill his contract that Jim Ach made to please the crowd, there would have been no disappointment."[9]

On Sunday afternoon and evening local dramatic societies presented two Czech plays in native tongue. Bad roads cut down the number but not the spirit of the audiences.

"During all three days the bazaar was in progress and meals were served in the basement. The total receipts from all sources have not yet been definitely determined, but they will not be far from the $3,000 mark. Hundreds of people were kept away by the rain and the condition of the roads. The management is considering repeating the two plays, giving one of them on one Sunday evening and the other the next Sunday evening. This would give our friends from a distance an opportunity to see the new hall and witness a demonstration of how it meets the needs of the community. Should this be determined upon, the final announcement will be made in a few days. In the meantime, the hectic days are over and the auditorium is formally dedicated."[10]

So Milligan reached another peak, took another step along the long road which is called progress. After the dedication was over life returned to normal again, and the people of Milligan let down and began to enjoy the fruits of their labor.

People cannot always live on the heights, nor is all community spirit exhibited there, although it is at these times of high achievement that the spirit of the community is most manifest. It finds expression also in its modern school, its seven blocks of paved streets, its water department, and its electric lights, which are no longer turned off at midnight. In the summer of 1930 the village board was negotiating with

---

° *Nebraska Signal*, May 1, 1930, p. 6.
¹° *Nebraska Signal*, May 1, 1930, p. 5.

two pipe line companies for the purpose of granting to one of them a gas franchise.

Such activities are the overt expressions of the hopes and the dreams, the likes and the dislikes of the people. To understand the attitude of the people toward the community in which they live, it is necessary to go' beyond the achievements of the past and explore the inner life in which they have their origin. Are the people satisfied with their past achievements? Of all that life in the community offers to them, what do they consider most worthwhile? What are their hopes and dreams for the future? What changes would they like to see effected in their community? The answers to these questions will complete the picture, and show more clearly the interaction between community and people.

Attitudes Toward the Community

On the whole the people of Milligan enjoy living in their community. Only 36 out of 470 Czechs said that they disliked living in Milligan. These individuals disliked it very much; none of them had a good word to say about the community. Twenty-seven of these lived in the village, and nine lived on the farms. Lesser contact with the community as a whole on the part of the farmer perhaps explains the difference. As long as the farmer has his farm, he is more or less indifferent to the village. Of those who disliked Milligan, 15 were members of the first generation, 19 belonged to the second, while but two belonged to the third. Of the 15 individuals of the first generation who disliked living in Milligan, 14 were in the age group forty and over, whereas but one was under forty. However, nearly all of the first-generation individuals living in Milligan belong to the age group forty and over. Of the 19 second-generation individuals who dislike Milligan, five were in the age group forty and over, 10 in the age group twenty-one to thirty-nine, and four were under twenty-one. Both of the third-generation individuals were in the age group twenty-one to thirty-nine. In terms of ages, 19 of the unsatisfied were forty or more, 13 were between twenty-one and thirty-nine, while four were under twenty-one.

A number of reasons were offered by these individuals for their dislike of Milligan. Some had lived in larger cities and did not like a small town. The older individuals found that the community had changed during the course of their lives, and they did not like what it had become. "There's too much American nonsense here now." The younger individuals did not like Milligan because it had not changed enough. "The

old people hang on too long. They don't give us a chance."
Some had transgressed the mores of the community, and
had felt the social disapproval which followed upon their
actions. Those who had been elsewhere examined the community with a critical eye; the older people who had gone
nowhere had seen the world come to Milligan and change its
life for the worse.

Among the non-Czechs the feeling was even stronger that
Milligan was not a desirable place in which to live. About
one-fifth of them could find nothing to praise. Three individuals reported that the only bond which held them to Milligan was their job. Seven were dissatisfied because they felt
themselves to be strangers living on alien soil. These individuals had made but a poor success of their lives, and perhaps would not have fitted in elsewhere. The community did
not accept them, and they returned hostility or indifference
with dislike.

Of the 470 Czechs who answered this question, 434 replied
that they liked to live in Milligan. Fourteen of them replied
that they did not know what they liked, while 15 replied that
they liked nothing best, but said that they liked to live in
Milligan. Thus 405 individuals remain who were able to tell
what they considered to be the best reason for living in Milligan. A few gave more than one, so that the total number of
reasons amounted to 438. About one-half of these replies
stressed the fact that Milligan was a desirable place in which
to live because of the many friends and relatives to be found
in the community. This reply was given by 216 individuals.
The next most important aspect of the community stressed
was the fact that Milligan was a Bohemian community.
These individuals liked Milligan because Bohemian people
lived here, and because there were Bohemian plays and entertainments. Forty-seven individuals made this reply. Twenty-
five belonged to the first generation, 15 to the second, and
seven to the third. In terms of ages, 32 were forty or more, 10
were between twenty-one and thirty-nine, and five were under
twenty-one. It is thus for the most part the older individuals
of the first and second generations who are pleased with
Milligan because it retains the culture of the old world.

An answer closely allied to the first group of answers
was made by 37 individuals. These liked best of all their
home or their farm. "My home and my children," or "My
farm," was the usual answer of this group.

Some 36 individuals found Milligan to be a community in
which good economic conditions prevailed. "Business and

business men are good." "I make a good living here." "The people pay their bills." "Farming is good here."

Another group, 32 in number, liked Milligan because of the entertainments and amusements offered by the community. "I like the new dance hall best." "There are a lot of dances held here." Only one of these individuals said that the moving picture show was the greatest attraction. Music and dancing were the types of entertainment mentioned with greatest frequency.

Sixteen individuals stressed Milligan's healthful climate. During the summer in which this investigation was made the temperature reached 100 degrees or more Fahrenheit daily during an uninterrupted period of six weeks. While he perspired so much that at times writing was difficult, the investigator was forced to write down statements such as "The climate is so healthy here." Marvelous indeed is the adaptability of man. Another group, 14 in number, found Milligan a good place for the nerves. They admired the quiet and peace of a small town.

A small group of individuals found in the qualities of the people living in the community the most commendable aspect of its life. Two of them liked the community spirit; three liked the people because they were contented and co-operative, while three liked them because they were independent.

Another small group liked Milligan for the associations which were found in the community. Five of them liked going to church, three enjoyed the lodge meetings, while one liked Milligan because it had a good school.

All of the other replies consisted of statements on any one of which not more than two people could agree. These miscellaneous reasons consisted of statements such as "Well off, don't worry"; "Living among people I know I can serve"; "Can cuss everybody"; "No social obligations"; "Don't have to attend church"; "Home cooking"; "Sitting on benches and talking and not having any work to do"; "Chance here for me to marry a widow I know"; "Hunting and fishing."

Except for the fact that the percentage of those who disliked to live in Milligan was greater among the non-Czechs than among the Czechs, the answers made by the two groups did not differ greatly. Forty of the 50 non-Czechs enjoyed living in Milligan, although four of them could not say why they liked it. Nineteen of them enjoyed living in Milligan because the people were sociable and friendly. Three liked it because it was a good community, but did not specify the aspects of the community life which they liked best. Sixteen other reasons were given, but on none of them could more than two individuals agree. Entertainments, good business conditions, climate, good conditions for farming, and the possession of a farm and home were mentioned. Other answers follow: "It's a clean little town"; "Everybody tends to his own business and people are not stuck up"; "It's a live, progressive town"; "I love nature and the life on the farm"; "There is more freedom here, and better food and health."

What the people as a whole think of their community is perhaps now clear. This knowledge, however, must be supplemented by the remarks of individual citizens. Some typical statements of Czechs follow:

"Of all I like best our new hall. I would like to have money to pay off the bonds on it. This is a Bohemian neighborhood; it grew up under our eyes. When one is used to a place he likes it. If one lived elsewhere he would like that place."

"I like it well. I like the social life, the friends and relatives. I liked to play in amateur theatricals. Until I was fifty-five I played the part of grandmother."

"I like nothing here. I have nothing here. If we only had a farm."

"At first I did not like it, but I'm used to it now. The people here are too curious."

"I like my friends and the folks. The people here stick together. They are sociable and friendly, more so than in any other town."

"I don't like living in Milligan. In a small town there is too much gossip. Too many people know your business."

"I like it because it is a Bohemian community, as much as it was before. The old folks don't think so, but I do."

"I don't know. I'm here because my husband is here. I like the social life of the people."

"I was born and raised here. There is no liking about it. I would miss my friends most."

"I know everybody. It seems we are all one family."

"I am at home here. My mother lives here. My husband makes his living here. I don't care much as long as he makes a living. I'd follow him anywhere. Here in Milligan, also, the children have a chance to learn Bohemian. Where we lived before we were the only Bohemian family and they did not learn Bohemian."

The statements of the non-Czechs differ somewhat:

"I like the Bohemian people; they are so friendly. Everyone greets me, even strangers. I missed my former friends and relatives at first."

"The people are nice to deal with. One could not find a finer class of people. I do not like the fact that people talk Bohemian when one visits them. Milligan has always had a bad name. Rough people from other towns come here on Sunday to entertainments and misbehave. This is a Christian nation and we should respect Sunday."

"I feel at home here. American people are harder to associate with. Bohemian people are more friendly and sociable."

"I don't like Milligan. I would rather be among my like."

Suggested Community Improvements

"What changes ought to be made in Milligan?" This question elicited a wide variety of answers. More than 80 different suggestions were made by the Czechs. The non-Czechs had but 17 suggestions to offer, but the number of non-Czechs in the community was much smaller than the number of Czechs. The suggestions may be classified under four heads: Civic improvements, economic improvements, social improvements, and moral improvements.

A rather large minority of the people, 195, believed that no changes were necessary. Many of these protested against the great number of changes which had occurred during recent years. They were especially distressed because village improvements had raised taxes to the point where they were considered unbearable. Others of this group believed that Milligan was perfect as it was. A few lived in the country and were not very familiar with conditions in the village.

A majority consisting of 275 Czechs believed that changes should be made, and offered a total of 386 points. Some 178 fell under the head of civic improvements, 86 under economic improvements, 67 under social improvements, and 49 under moral improvements. Six individuals believed that some changes should be made, but could not state specifically what they were.

Among civic improvements five received the votes of more than 10 individuals. Thirty-nine believed that Milligan needed a swimming pool, 28 that the streets, alleys, and roads needed improvement, 27 that the village needed a better water supply, 15 that the children needed more playground equipment, and 21 that brick buildings should replace the wooden buildings which remained on Main Street. Other suggestions, none of which received more than four votes, were such as the following: A sewer system; improved street lights; better parking facilities; nicer homes and yards; a better schoolhouse and grounds; more parks; more homes. Two individuals desired a golf course, one a tennis court, one a skating rink, and one more sports for girls. As the study was made during a very hot summer, the need of a swimming pool was uppermost in the minds of the people. Also, the drought had made it necessary to use a well which gave water that was quite salty. Objections were raised to some improvements which would prove of interest to children. "What do we need a new swimming pool for? The water in the creek is purer than the water in a swimming pool would be." "Why should children get playground equipment? We never had any in our day, and we amused ourselves."

Economic conditions were quite bad in Nebraska in the summer of 1930. Agriculture had been in a depressed state ever since the boom days of the war, and prices of agricultural products had been falling steadily. A great many suggestions for improvement were offered by the people of Milligan, but only two received more than five votes. Twenty-four individuals believed that Milligan would be much better off if a factory were built there. Almost as large a number, 22, believed that all would be well if the saloon returned. Five individuals believed that the town needed another railroad, while one believed that bus service would be a great improvement. Four individuals believed that the town needed an airport, two that it needed a new hotel, four that it needed new stores, one that it needed a better bank, one that it needed better barbers, and one that Milligan should capitalize on its salty water supply and become a health resort. Two believed that all business should be on a cash basis. Lower taxes attracted the votes of three. Two individuals thought that working hours were too long in Milligan, and should be limited. Several others voted for an improvement in economic conditions, without specifying what should be done.

Suggested social improvements included educational and recreational changes, and those which would result in better health. The largest number of votes, 24, were cast for a public library. Fourteen individuals thought that the school system would be improved if more courses were offered. Seven individuals thought that the community would be improved if the Czech language were used more and if Czech customs prevailed to a greater extent than they did. "We need more Bohemian 'stuff' here in Milligan." Two individuals believed that more Sokol meetings should be held in Milligan. Four voted for a good theatre, three for better movies, one for a good music instructor, and one for community singing. One thought that a hospital would help, and one that Milligan needed a better doctor. Two were concerned with the young; one believed they needed a director of athletics, and the other that they needed proper amusement. Several were not very specific, but believed that there should be a development of social intercourse.

Moral improvements received the least number of votes, 49. However, feeling ran rather high among those who advocated moral improvements. One could advocate an economic or civic improvement with a placid countenance, but when a moral improvement was suggested a bitter expression usually appeared on the speaker's face. Eleven votes were cast in favor of ridding the town of bootleggers and drinking. Eight individuals voted in favor of fewer dances, and the same number believed that Milligan needed a Protestant church. Four individuals believed that life would be much better if everybody minded his own business, and a like number that community life would be improved if people loved one another. Three individuals believed that the community needed a new building for its Catholic Church. Two people believed that the town needed better leaders; men who could broaden small people. The following statements were each made by a single individual: "There should be education in morals and character given by the Sokols"; "Children should be better taken care of"; "People should have higher ideals and they should go to church"; "Loafing benches should be removed from Main Street"; "Better etiquette, with less swearing"; "Should be fewer lodges"; "More people should vote and clean up things"; "The loudspeaker on Main Street should be silenced"; "Should be no school."

Among the non-Czechs the proportion of those who did not recommend any changes was about the same as it was among the Czechs. Thirty-one individuals had 35 suggestions to offer. Most of the suggestions were the same as those made by the Czechs, but among the non-Czechs a majority emphasized the need for moral improvement. Twelve of the 31 believed that Milligan's greatest need was a strong Protestant church, while two believed that the inhabitants should show greater respect for Sunday. One believed that there should be a greater mixture of blood, and three that the people should speak more English than they did. Ten suggested civic improvements; seven social improvements, and three economic improvements.

Some typical quotations from Czechs follow:

"That the people should be better than they are. Everybody is for himself. Everybody should be together."

"Playground equipment and a swimming pool. The people should have higher ideals. They should go to church on Sunday."

"The town ought to be a little more progressive. We need a town board that would get more improvements, such as gravel for the streets. The town ought to get all the loafing benches from in front of the stores along Main Street. There are too many elderly loafers there. They want to be respected and looked up to. Men in Milligan retire after they are forty and loaf the rest of their lives."

"Cut out the swearing. More etiquette is needed. The majority of people don't have it, though the better classes do."

"None. Better heads would know."

"Beer. Old people would be happy. Taxes are too high. There have been too many improvements. People die in the fields. They have no beer."

"People here start things and don't finish them. The leaders are mistaken. A few men stick together and the rest have no say-so. We want a walk across the street and it hasn't been put in yet, while other improvements are made."

"I don't see how Milligan could be better."

"None. Everything is just about right now. All we need is a good hard rain."

Some suggestions made by non-Czechs follow:

"A little more religion brought into the community and less of worldly entertainment."

"Get all American people that could get in. Too many Bohemians."

"A few more churches. The people are too worldly. They don't think of anything but pleasure. The world in general is too worldly. It don't think of the hereafter. If there was more religion there would be fewer suicides and crimes."

"Some Protestant church ought to be put into the town. A minister there has no audience. They have run Sunday Schools out of town more than once."

"I can't say much against Milligan. It is very progressive. It needs no immediate improvements."

"They ought to build a good big Protestant church there."

Only a few answers have been given; enough to show how the community affects the individual. A community may be one, but the individuals composing it are many, and each is affected in a slightly different way by his contact with its life. Some find much to praise; others are indifferent to the community, while a few would have it changed to suit their individual needs and desires. Those whose lives are successful usually find the community a good place in which to live. The introverts pay but little attention to the community, and live pretty largely in a world of their own creation. Those who have nothing to conceal do not resent the prying eyes of their neighbors, and regard them as friends rather than foes. Those who have transgressed the mores of the community attempt unsuccessfully to hide their transgressions, and deplore the inquisitiveness and curiosity of their neighbors. Some of the non-Czechs feel that the community would be better if it were more American, while some of the older Czechs believe that it has advanced too far from the folkways and mores brought over from the old world.

When the Czechs of Milligan thought of improvements which ought to be made their minds turned generally to some economic or civic change which would make community life better. But when they were asked to tell what they liked best about living in Milligan, their minds did not turn generally to the many improvements in their material life which had already been made. These improvements gave them some joy, no doubt, but they had lived without them and they could live without them again. The element in their lives which they found most satisfying, and without which their lives would cease to have meaning or purpose, was the network of social relationships into which they had entered. The non-Czechs in Milligan emphasized the necessity for changes in the inner rather than in the outer world because the inner world in which they lived was not satisfying. The non-Czechs who were most dissatisfied were those who had not established satisfactory social relationships with those who lived about them. They felt themselves to be living among people who were foreign to them. Why did they so much emphasize the need for more religion in Milligan? When the world of social relationships is unsatisfactory the world of spiritual relationships is inviting and serves to quiet some of the yearnings which cannot be appeased in the world of men. Perhaps they hoped that by calling people to God they would also draw them closer to themselves.

Also, in their early life they had received a great deal of religious training. Individuals who were without this training were different, and they found it difficult to understand them and associate with them.

Analysis of Changes

This modern age is dominated perhaps by the philosophy of materialism, and too much importance is attached to the possession of material things. There is a certain joy in creation, whether it be a work of art or a machine. The world has set its feet on the pathway of progress, and struggles blindly on toward unrealized goals. Milligan is not free of these urges, and prides itself on being a progressive town. It has its great moments, when it feels that it has attained some of the heights, when it is sure that it is marching steadily on the road to progress. If the aviator mentioned earlier in this chapter had passed over Milligan on purebred sire day, he might have exclaimed, "Ah! Now the people live." He would have been mistaken. The people were not living; they were acting. They were being moved by forces and influences which came to them from beyond the broad fields which lie about them. The great moments are not the periods when people experience the greatest satisfaction. It is in the small moments which make up the daily round of their existence that the people really live. It is in the social relationships in which they live day after day that they find their greatest satisfaction. If these are destroyed, life ceases. When death comes life ends for the living as well as for the dead. Man finds his life in the social relationships in which he lives, and when one of these is terminated by the death of a friend or relative, a part of one's life ends with the death of the loved one.[11]

What conclusions, then, may be drawn with respect to the community and the people who compose it? In the first place, the community is relatively harmonious. It satisfies in pretty large measure the needs and desires of those who live in it. They have built it, and they are satisfied with their creation. Here in America the Czechs have found freedom to build as they desired. In the old world the people could enter into social relationships with their neighbors, but these relationships were limited. The people were restricted to a narrow circle of friends and relatives, and occupied the lower rungs of the social scale. The social relationships into which they entered gave them great satisfaction, and they missed

[11] Cf. R. M. MacIver, *Society, Its Structure and Changes* (New York, 1931), Chapter II.

them severely when they left the old world. In the half century which has passed since the first settlers arrived the inhabitants have built a community which more nearly reflects their needs and desires than did that in which they lived in the old world. There is some friction between Czechs and non-Czechs, and between the earlier generations and the later. The non-Czechs are dissatisfied because the community does not represent the type to which they were accustomed, and they feel that they have but little control over their destinies. The old feel that the community is changing, and that control has passed out of their hands. Whatever happiness the individual finds in life is determined pretty largely by the control which he has over it. Immigrants in cities are often maladjusted because they lack control over their lives; they are moved and influenced by forces which lie beyond them. This is not true in an isolated agricultural village where 90 per cent of the individuals are of the same nationality.

Today Milligan is no longer as isolated as it was. It is subjected to influences from without, and its community life is changing. The younger are more responsive to these changes than are the older people, and are more ready to adopt the new and displace the old. However, the old remains. The "day" and the "week" are American inventions, but even on purebred sire day there were many evidences of the old world. It is probable that changes in the future will come so slowly as not to disturb the harmony of the community life.

In the second place, the very harmony of the community life makes it impossible to hold all of its members.[12] The individuals who react most to outside influences find it impossible to remain. The ambitious young find it difficult to adjust themselves to the slowly changing community. The older people still have a fairly firm grip on things. The past still lives. Security rather than adventure is the dominant wish of many of the inhabitants. Some of the eager youth desire adventure, and leave their homes to seek it. As a result, disturbing elements are eliminated, and the life of the community flows on in tranquillity and peace.

---

[12] See age distribution in Introduction.

CHAPTER XII

IN CONCLUSION

Summary

A half century or more ago the first settlers filtered into the area which was later to give birth to Milligan. The first to come secured homesteads, and knew all of the hardships of life on the frontier. These first immigrants left a Bohemia of fertile land and great natural resources. However, the political and social system which prevailed there prevented them from receiving the benefits of this rich country. The nobles and the wealthy landowners controlled the best land.

Some of the more fortunate peasants were able to secure good land. These found life in Bohemia satisfactory, and did not migrate. On the other hand, the laborers who worked for others and owned no land did not possess capital enough to migrate, and hence remained in Bohemia. Individuals who belonged to the small-cottager class possessed a little land, but not enough to support them comfortably. These had capital enough to pay their passage to the new world, and sold what little they possessed and came to America. Many of the inhabitants of Milligan said that they came to America because they found nothing but poverty in Bohemia. Families were large, and opportunities for advancement were few.

However, while economic factors were among the chief reasons for migration, there were other contributing conditions. The government was in the control of the German Hapsburgs. The Czechs were limited at every hand by the Austrian state. Bohemia was a land of political oppression as well as of economic misery. The Catholic Church supported the Austrian state and was in turn supported by the government. It was impossible for the people to worship as they chose. Again, compulsory military training meant that the men were forced to leave their homes in the prime of life and give service to a state which they hated.

While the state did oppress the people, it did not deprive them of an education. By the middle decades of the nineteenth century education was universal and compulsory. However, this was true only of elementary education. The "gymnasium" and the university were still restricted to the few. It was impossible to rise into the higher social classes without higher education. Hence, here again, the lives of the people were limited.

It was to escape these limitations that people migrated to the new world. Those who settled in American cities found the physical adjustment easy, the social adjustment hard; those who went to the new states on the frontier found the physical adjustment rather difficult at first, and the social adjustment almost impossible because of the lack of community life. The soil was hard and unyielding; droughts and grasshoppers ruined the crops. Many could not endure the physical hardships, and went to the cities, where they worked at trades.

However, the physical hardships were not the worst feature of life on the plains. In Bohemia the people lived in village communities; in America on isolated farms. The lack of community life was almost unbearable. At this time the hard work that was necessary to break the soil was a blessing rather than a hardship, because it made the people forget their loneliness.

During pioneer days schools were few and poor. The boys and girls were needed on the farm at an early age. As a result, many of those who were born in the new world at this time attended school so little that they never learned the English language. Whatever education they obtained was secured in the home, and the old world culture was passed on almost without change. Thus there are found in Milligan today some citizens who were born in the new world, but who really belong to the old.

As the years passed educational facilities improved. Today the school rather than the home educates the children. As a result, the old culture is losing out to the new. The school is a typical American product, and subtly Americanizes its pupils. The Czech language is disappearing; the young attend college in increasing numbers and pass out into the general life of America.

In Europe many of the immigrants had been skilled or semi-skilled laborers; in the new world they could find but little opportunity to practice their trades. Only blacksmiths and harness makers were in demand. These had an opportunity to work at their crafts in addition to farming, and were often able to make more money than those who engaged in no other occupation than farming. In Europe differentiation of occupation was largely on the basis of production. In the new community a differentiation of occupations based largely on trade developed as the community grew. Today this differentiation has proceeded as far as it can go. There is no room for more stores in Milligan. However, there are many, especially among the young, who would like to work and cannot find a job. A factory would solve this problem, and a factory the people would like to have. However, there is no one with sufficient enterprise or capital within the community to start such a factory. The isolated position of Milligan, off the main line of the railroad as it is, makes the project difficult. Hence, the surplus population finds it necessary to leave. Some go to undeveloped sections in the United States, where they buy farms. Others go to the cities, where they find work in factories or trades. Some attend college and enter business or professional life.

In the Bohemia from which the immigrants came there was little emphasis on progress. The Milligan of today prides itself on being a very progressive town. The Chamber of Commerce is ever on the lookout for some new activity in which it may engage. Its projects call for much co-operation on the part of the people, and its activities result in the development of community spirit. The community is bound together in these common tasks.

While the members of the community take great pride in the material progress displayed, their greatest satisfaction comes from the social relationships into which they enter.

It is in the family and home that the strongest social relationships are formed. In Milligan, as in Bohemia, the home is a very important element in the life of the individual. The family in Milligan bears a greater resemblance to the patriarchal family of the old world than it does to the more highly evolved association to be found in urban communities. A few of its functions have been taken away, but many still remain. The one agency in the community which has succeeded in taking away from the family a function which was very important in pioneer days is the public school. Education is now carried on in the public school. This has resulted in considerable change occurring in the community. Children are brought up in American rather than in Czech folkways. However, the family still exercises a great influence. Most of the children learn the Czech language at home. Nearly all of the social life of the community centers about the home. The family is a conservative influence, and tends to slow up the process of change.

Youth and age dwell together in Milligan in relative harmony. There are some objections raised to the behavior of the young, but on the whole these are objections which might be raised by the elders in any American community. The elders have had control over the community life which was built. There has been exerted little pressure to make them American citizens. They have been able to work out an adjustment to American life which is satisfactory to them. They have developed but few feelings of inferiority. Meanwhile, because no pressure has been exerted, the first-generation members have absorbed a great deal of American culture. They left the old world so long ago that they have forgotten about it. The community in which they live is the only one they have ever really known. The community and the family have created the children, not exactly in the image of the elders, but not so different from them as to make the community life inharmonious.

In Bohemia the Czechs belonged to the Catholic Church, not from desire but because of necessity. In Milligan three-fourths of the Czech people do not belong to any church. Those who do belong to a church are more likely to attend the Catholic Church than the Protestant. The Protestant church in Milligan suffers especially from the fact that it is in the control of the non-Czechs, who do not understand the temperament of the Czech people. Bohemians are not so much anti-religious as they are anti-clerical. The Catholic Church in Bohemia went beyond its natural sphere and interfered in worldly affairs to the detriment of the Czech people. The opposition to the Catholic Church is based as much on political grounds as on religious. The activities of the Catholic Church in Bohemia engendered such a hatred of all churches on the part of the Czechs as to drive many of them to the extreme left wing in matters of religion. In America, where no one is compelled to attend the church, the Czechs have thus far remained outside its doors. In the future, perhaps, as church leaders learn to understand the Czech people and send to them ministers who know how to deal with them, they may once more find it desirable to become church members. If the church will not concern itself with the things that are Caesar's, but confine its attention to the things of God, the Czechs will have little objection to it. The antagonism which was characteristic of the early Czech immigrants to America has been replaced by indifference. It is only when some zealous, but misguided individual such as Father Verhelst comes to Milligan that the still waters are stirred. After the departure of Father Verhelst, the pool became quiet again, and continues so today.

Leisure-time activities in Milligan show many evidences of old and new. A great deal of reading matter published in the Czech language is still received in Milligan, but this material decreases year by year, as the older people die off. Community visiting exists in Milligan much as it does in a village of the old world. The sense of community is much stronger in Milligan than it is in the average open-country neighborhood in the United States. Of all the programs which the radio brings to Milligan, none is enjoyed more than those which feature Bohemian music. The food which is served in the household is still primarily Czech. Thus in the activities which may be grouped under the head of unorganized leisure, there is a great deal of evidence of the culture of the old world.

In those aspects of its leisure-time life which have been organized, there is more evidence of the new than of the old. An association expresses the attitudes and ideals of its members. It arises out of the conditions found in the group life of the community. When those conditions change, the association must change. When the particular need which called the association into being disappears, the association either disappears or changes so radically as to lose its former identity. The Sokol organization, founded to meet certain conditions in Bohemia, was brought over to America by the early immigrants. In Europe this organization had two purposes; first, the improvement of the mental and physical health of its members; and second, the creation of an independent Bohemia. In the early days of immigration the Sokol organization was very powerful in Czech communities in America. Most of its members had belonged to the association in the old world. It was striving hard to further the independence of Bohemia, and this aroused much enthusiasm and gained it many members. Also, the Sokol hall was a place where congenial people could gather and have a good time. In this period Czechs knew little English, and could find entertainment only among their own people. The drills and exhibitions, in which old and young, male and female, strong and weak, could take part, gave the members an opportunity to satisfy their desire for recognition.

For all of these reasons the Sokol organization grew and prospered. However, conditions changed, and today, the association is losing out in importance and prestige. Bohemia has won its independence, and there is no need for missionary work to further the cause. The early members are old; many of them have died, and those who live can no longer engage in strenuous physical exercise. The second- and third-generation individuals speak the English language, and mingle with American groups. Modern sports, such as basketball, baseball, tennis, and golf attract them more than do the types of exercises offered by the Sokols. To some extent the Sokols are trying to attract the young by introducing these sports, but the leaders of the organization are old men who see with the eyes of the old world.

It is difficult to predict the future of the organization accurately, but it is certain that it will be no longer the important agency in preserving the culture of the old world it was in the past. It may disappear entirely, although this is unlikely. More probably, it will either retain its old characteristics and appeal to a small and conservative group among the people, or it will change and become essentially an American athletic club. In any case, it will be unimportant as an agency of cultural preservation.

So, likewise, with the Czech lodge. Founded by the early immigrants, it has been a very important agency in the preservation of the culture of the old world. But today it finds that the young do not care to belong to an organization in which most of the business is carried on in the Czech language, and in which all the important offices are held by men who were born in Bohemia many years ago. Hence, English-speaking lodges are organized, and younger men and women, born in America, are encouraged to join them. The character of the lodge is changing; it is today not as much interested in the preservation of the old-world culture as it is in self-preservation. As conditions change, the organization must change. It has not yet found itself, but when it does, the old zeal for the preservation of Czech culture in America will be greatly diminished.

On the other hand, organizations which were founded in the new world are likely to be instrumentalities of change. Thus the woman's club, an essentially American organization, holds meetings at which programs are presented which have little to do with the old world. Indeed, in the programs from time to time some attempt is made to stress the culture of America. The same is true of children's clubs.

Thus, leisure-time organizations in Milligan often act as agencies through which influences causing cultural change play upon the community. On the other hand, in that part of the leisure time which is unorganized, the culture of the old world is able to survive more easily.

During the nineteenth century a wave of nationalism swept over Europe. Bohemia was not immune to this influence, and awoke from the long sleep of political inactivity which succeeded the Thirty Years War. About the middle of the century an attempt was made to wring concessions from the King, but these failed, and many of those who were active in the abortive attempt to make Bohemia free were forced to flee the country. The long struggle for independence which began at this time made the people politically conscious.

This political consciousness was lost in the new world. The inhabitants of Milligan are Republicans and Democrats, without knowing much about either of the parties. By this time it has become a habit with most of the people to vote the regular ticket, which they and their parents before them have voted. The granting of suffrage to women has not changed conditions much, as the women vote as do their menfolk. Most of the members of the community are reconciled to women's suffrage, but a few of the old-timers still think that the woman's place is in the home. A few blame women for bringing in prohibition; a few believe that the hard times which have come in recent years are due to the fact that women were granted the suffrage. For the most part, however, the people of Milligan are indifferent to politics. The only time any great interest is shown is when someone from the community runs for a political office, or when economic conditions change seriously for the worse. In political affairs, Milligan is very much like any American community.

Urban versus Rural Immigrant Adjustment

Old and new combine in the community life of Milligan in varying degrees. In the large cities of America such combinations give rise to conflicts and social problems. Many of the problems which perplex the large city are believed to be caused by the fact that they contain large masses of unassimilable immigrants. Another causative factor is said to be the fact that certain types of city environment create certain sociological types. Thus the "interstitial area" is the birthplace of the gang, the "gas-house district" the seat of crime.

These factors no doubt possess some importance. However, the large city is too new an element in our modern life for easy determination of the causes which lie back of its difficulties. The doors of the city have not been closed, and until they are it will be impossible to determine which of its problems are indigenous to its life and which are problems of migration.[1] It is migration, as much as immigration, which is responsible for the unpleasant plight of the immigrant in the city. His daily life represents a clash between city and country, as well as the conflict of two national cultures. His woes are often many, and his life is hard, as this description of the Czech community in Chicago shows.

"Parental control often breaks down where the parents readily give up their native heritages and do not educate their children to respect them. This is, however, less frequently the main trouble and cause of future difficulties. The influence of environment, companionship,

---

[1] Cf. R. M. MacIver, *Society, Its Structure and Changes* (New York, 1931), Chapter XIX.

American public schools, especially where the teachers are prejudiced against the nationality of parents, and allow ridicule or where they are unintelligent and do not understand the social and cultural environment in which the children live, are almost always more to blame for disrespect to parents, disobedience, and later on, moral laxity and irresponsibility and very often, when the children grow up, for crime.

"I am perfectly conscious of this heavy indictment. I would not blame the American teachers for it. It is the fault of the whole heavy, suffocating atmosphere that hangs over and overshadows the foreign settlements and neighborhoods of all large American cities. The land of the disinherited, in the full social and cultural sense of the word. There is a great and painful feeling of shame, shame of one's own origin, shame of one's own name, shame of one's nationality, shame of one's mother tongue, shame for everything that is dearest to us, a terrible monster of this social shame stares at you from every corner in the street, from the depressed faces of the men and women that you meet on the sidewalk and from the eyes of the bigger school children playing in front of their tenement homes, from every window and from every eye that you see. I am afraid to say it, but I cannot help the feeling that this is worse than a reversion to barbarism.

"Respect for parents, respect for old men and women, love of friends, loyalty to one's race are the old virtues of mankind, tested in the crucible of the past struggles for generations, and they still remain the pillars of modern society. What is it that takes their places, after they are spoiled, ridiculed, downtrodden with shame?"[2]

No one could ever describe Milligan in these words. In Milligan as in the community portrayed above the people are Czech, coming from the same sort of environment in the old world. No heavy, suffocating atmosphere hangs over Milligan; no feelings of shame trouble the minds of its inhabitants. The community life is harmonious, the people are contented and happy. Why is there this great difference between the two communities? The Czech who settled in Chicago came from a country to a city environment. "Respect for parents, respect for old men and women, love of friends, and loyalty to one's race" are the virtues and ideals of the country-side, where the family is all-powerful. In the city the immigrants found people living in what Dr. Muller-Lyer has called the social-individual stage.[3] The patriarchal family of the old world was assailed on every hand by the individualistic tendencies of city life. A great deal of the pain involved in adjustment to the city was due to this factor.

In Milligan, on the other hand, the people live in a country environment, which resembles in many respects that which they knew in the old world. The family is a very powerful influence; much of the lives of the people are still passed

[2] Jakub Horak, *op. cit.*, pp. 48, 49.
[3] Dr. F. Muller-Lyer, *The Family* (New York, 1931).

within its confines and its ideals are still very influential in
the life of the community.

Again, in Chicago the Czechs had but little control over
their lives. Dr. Horak blames the public school for turning
children against parents and creating feelings of inferiority
in the inhabitants of foreign settlements. In Chicago the
Czechs could not control the public school. They did not
choose the teachers, nor did they prescribe what should be
taught. In Milligan, on the other hand, the people of the
community do choose the teachers, and, within limits, they
may prescribe what should be taught. It is not necessary to
stipulate the exact details of the subject matter. The attitude of the teacher is more important in the creation of mental patterns than the subject he teaches. No teacher in Milligan would last long if he tried to ridicule the individuals
who live in the community. Contracts are renewable yearly,
and teachers are very careful to cater to the opinions of the
community.

Thus, in the city the social environment is complex; in
the country it is simple. In the city the immigrant comes into
contact with many phases of life, in the country with but
few. In the city are many different nationalities, and many
different social classes. In Milligan ninety per cent of the
people are Czech; all the people are farmers or depend directly
on farmers for their livelihood. In the city the social structure is highly differentiated; in the country there are few
associations and life is pretty largely lived in primary groups.

An immigrant going from a country environment in the
old world to a country environment in the new world will be
able to make the necessary adjustment without much difficulty. This was especially true of the adjustment which the
immigrant made to the conditions found in Milligan after
the community had been formed. In pioneer days the lack
of community experienced by the early settlers was a condition vastly different from those to be found in the old world,
and caused them much suffering. However, in the long run
this condition benefitted the settlers, for it allowed them to
build the community to conform to their own desires and
ideals. The community which was built was not greatly
different from that which the settlers had known in the old
world.

Those Czechs who settled in country districts in America were thus going from one environment to another which
did not differ greatly from that which they had known. The
new environment was but little more dynamic than the old.
Social life in agricultural areas the world over changes very

slowly, whereas, in urban communities it is subject to a bewildering process of change.

When the immigrant goes from his village in the old world to a great city in the new, he finds that he must make, not one great adjustment, after which all will be peace, but that he will be forced to make new adjustments during all the remaining days of his life. The first adjustment, made when the immigrant comes to the new world, might be termed a horizontal adjustment, a change from one plane of living to another. He soon finds that he has moved, not only from one plane of living to another, but also that he has moved from a static world into a dynamic one. In the new world there are no fixed places, as there were in the old. Everything changes and the immigrant must go through a continuous process of adjustment. This creates many problems which are not found if the immigrant to America has settled on the land, where life is relatively static, and where such changes as occur are more completely under the control of the individuals who live in the community.

Social Changes and Social Trends in Milligan

While adjustment is easier in the country than it is in the city, it would not be true to say that the community of Milligan has no problems or that the social life of the community has not changed. However, the problems are never very acute, and there is no great necessity to solve them immediately. The social life of the community is relatively balanced, and the friction that arises from time to time is never so great as to endanger the communal solidarity.

As far as the changes are concerned, it is easier to describe them than to discover their causes. Undoubtedly, one of the factors responsible for the changes is the greater differentiation of the social structure today. The school has taken over the job of educating the children, and the school introduces new ideas into the life of the community. Outside associations affect the community through such organizations as the woman's club. Meanwhile, the changes which are made in the minds of the people by such organizations as these in turn affect those associations which try to preserve the culture of the old world. The young people in the community have been taught a different way of life, and demand that the organizations controlled by the elders change to conform to the new point of view.

Milligan has now been subjected to the sociological microscope, and stands revealed as a society in which many strands are intertwined. Some of these threads are centuries old, and were spun by people who have long since passed away. Others are new, and were made by individuals who are still active in the life of the community. The pattern which has been woven is unique. Are the people who make up the community satisfied with their handiwork, and is the pattern of social life better than that which is to be found in the old world? These are questions which involve valuations and cannot be answered scientifically. However, it is possible to point out what has been gained and lost in the course of the migration from the old world to the new.

In the first place, the inhabitants of the community possess greater wealth than they would have possessed if they had remained in Bohemia. Many of them left the old world to escape from poverty, and most of them have achieved this objective. The plains of Nebraska were not paved with gold, but the fertile fields rewarded well those who toiled and saved. However, in recent years the farmers have come to realize that their prosperity is bound up with that of the world as a whole. Agricultural prices have been falling ever since the World War, and the position of the farmer has become increasingly insecure. There was poverty in the old world, it is true, but there was no depression. Or, perhaps, there was a continuous depression. One of the farm laborers in Milligan said that he left Bohemia because of poverty there, but he was not so sure but that he was worse off in America now than he would have been had he remained in Bohemia.

Again, in America the immigrants have found more freedom than they ever had in the old world. Church and State in Bohemia restricted the liberties of the people. In the United States everyone is equal before the law, and each individual may worship or not as he pleases.

In Bohemia the classes were sharply drawn, and there was but little opportunity to rise into a higher social level. In Milligan cultural opportunities are open to all, and the station which the individual occupies is determined by his own efforts rather than by birth.

On the whole, the people of Milligan are certain that they have gained rather than lost by coming to the new world. They are not completely satisfied, and there are many things they would like to change. They would not be Czechs if they found everything to their liking. They feel that their destinies lie in their own hands here, whereas, in Bohemia their lives were determined for them by others.

Before leaving the people of Milligan, it would be well to analyze the changes which have occurred in the past in order to determine the trends in the social life of the community. As is usually the case in culture conflicts, the ways and means, the external side of life, have yielded more readily than the inner values, the ends of existence. In outward appearance Milligan does not differ from the average American village. The houses are built to the conventional pattern, and their rooms are filled with the typical products of the machine age. However, the people in their American clothing may speak only in the Czech tongue. The latest model radio may adorn the family living room, but remain silent except when an orchestra is broadcasting Bohemian music. The housewife may use a modern electric stove, but the food she prepares is the same as that which pleased her ancestors in some little village in Bohemia.

But even these persistent cultural traits manifest a trend toward disappearance. Preservation of the old-world culture would have been possible only if the people had settled in a region which was completely isolated. Relatively great persistence of a particular type of social life is found only in communities which are isolated either geographically, as in the mountains of Kentucky or Virginia, or socially, as in the case of Chinese settlements in New York or San Francisco. In the former communities there is ignorance of other societies, and therefore, but little feeling of social inferiority. In groups which suffer from social isolation there is usually developed a consciousness of inferiority.

When the first Czechs came to the Milligan area they may have been subjected to some degree of social isolation, but this disappeared as the community began to fill with people from Bohemia. There is today no feeling of inferiority on the part of the inhabitants. In the early years Milligan was isolated geographically, and the community life changed but slowly. In recent years improvements in transportation and communication have tended to integrate Milligan into the life of the greater community. As a result the social life is changing more rapidly today. The old ways are dying out, and some day perhaps the old Czech family names will be the sole reminders of Bohemia. Milligan, "the Bohemian town with the Irish name," will have become Milligan, "the American town with a Bohemian past."

VITA

Born Chicago, Illinois, November 11, 1899.
Attended University of Nebraska, 1919–1921;
Western Reserve University, 1921–February,
1923; Columbia University, February to June,
1923, summer sessions, 1924–1925, 1928–1931.
A. B., Western Reserve, 1923; A. M., Columbia,
1925. Publications: *Manual of Cleveland* (Cleveland, 1927).